Principles and Promises

Stepping Stones to the Kingdom

Larry H. Peer

Library of Congress Control Number: 2003107300
ISBN: 1-932280-14-6

This book is dedicated to Janet Priday Peer
and a striving family

Principles and Promises

CONTENTS

Principles and Promises

Introduction

As a practicing member of the Church of Jesus Christ of Latter-day Saints with many years of experience in other nationalities, cultures, language traditions, creeds, age groups, attitudes, and biases, I have found myself increasingly uneasy with the dilemma expressed by so many acquaintances and colleagues in my Church and others, as well as those not affiliated with any religion, about how to live righteously and happily in a world increasingly at odds with any kind of substantial value commitment, a distempered world of moral mediocrity and preposterous subjectivism. This distemper could be cured if we would

> ...turn for help to the larger domain, of which the material is but a faint reflection. Out of the unseen world comes a body of laws... these laws are as real and comprehensible as any physical law. If a wire carrying an electric current is placed above a mariner's compass, the needle swings sharply to one side, and remains there. Just so, obedience to any of the moral laws will determine and hold the actions of the man under that law. The acceptance or rejection of these moral or spiritual laws, higher laws of God, determine in fact the behavior and conduct of every human being... the moral laws, if sincerely and properly used, give power to solve life's problems. Above all else, conformity to them gives men conquest over themselves. (John A. Widtsoe, *Conference Reports,* October 1948 110–11)

In contemplating my own role as husband, father, friend, colleague, and general citizen of the world, I have found my mind returning again and again to a dozen ideas that are constantly at the core of conversations, concerns, and attempted explanations of successful living. Now, what I present here is not a scholarly volume: I write as I would speak in a conversation. Too, this book is not a publication of the Church of Jesus Christ of Latter-day Saints, and although I am solely responsible for its contents, I trust that thoughts on these particular Gospel virtues will be understood as one approach to a more successful way of dealing with basic ideas than the world's relativism allows. Anyone interested in more extensive discussions of the Gospel itself will find any number of powerful books and essays on the subject, beginning with many of the items listed in the works cited list at the end of this volume.

Idea One: INTEGRITY

Choose Ye This Day Whom Ye Will Be

The prophet Joshua admonished the people of the covenant by saying "choose you this day whom ye will serve: but as for me and my house, we will serve the Lord"(Joshua 24:15). All good and decent members of the Church seek to serve the Lord, but there is often something that interferes with our efforts, and makes it as difficult to serve as though we were inactive or not members at all. President Spencer W. Kimball said that we must "seek to understand that total honesty is a prerequisite for exaltation" (1980–81 *Melchizedek Priesthood Manual,* 164), and President McKay asserted

> Integrity is the first step to true greatness. Men love to praise, but are slow to practice, integrity. To maintain it in high places costs self-denial. In all places it is liable to opposition but its end is glorious, and the universe will yet do it homage. (*True to the Faith,* 129)

It is because all gospel virtues are rooted in integrity and spiritual maturity that this book begins with this concept. Without integrity we certainly cannot serve well and, in fact, we cannot serve at all. Furthermore, without integrity surely we shall find personal heartache and sorrow.

I

In this regard consider the famous story told by Sarah Pomeroy about the prophet Joseph Smith. She says

> Joseph requested my father to lend him $100 to pay the lawyer who defended Porter Rockwell. Father freely counted out the money. "This shall be returned within three days, if I am alive"' said the prophet, and departed. My aunt was (very upset with this). "Don't you know, Thomas," said she, "you will never see a cent of that money again. Here (is) your family without a home and now you throw your money away." (This was very serious to my child's mind) but I had faith that he would (pay it back). The day came when it was to be paid. A cold, wet, rainy day. The day passed. Night came. (It got late) and we retired for the night. Shortly after there was a knock at the door. Father arose and went to it, and there in the driving rain (and bitter cold) stood the prophet Joseph. "Here, Brother Thomas, is the money." (He counted out one hundred dollars in gold). Brother Joseph said, "Thomas, I have been trying all day to raise this sum, for my honor was at stake. God bless you." (And he departed into the night). (*Young Woman's Journal*, December 1906, 539)

This episode reveals the key: when all we do and all we say, even down to the tiniest things, is done with a full consciousness that our personal honor is at stake, we are ready for integrity. Perhaps we ought to be concerned about ourselves, our families, friends and neighbors, and fellow citizens in the kingdom of God in this regard. We need be neither cynical nor pessimistic; but one might wonder how much diamond-hard integrity there is in our world. Of course, there is *some* honor everywhere, but we might ask if that honor is at the level and according to the detail and intensity that Christ expects. Do we as individuals and family members insist upon this level of integrity in ourselves and others?

President Kimball taught some years ago that

> Today is the day to preach honesty and integrity. Many people have seemingly lost their concept of the God-given law of honesty...We find ourselves rationalizing in all forms of dishonesty...(A lack of integrity) comes in (many) forms; in...playing upon private emotions for filthy lucre; in robbing money tills or stealing commodities of employers; in falsifying accounts; in taking advantage of other taxpaying people by misuse of food stamps and (by making) false claims; in taking unreal exemptions; in taking out government or private loans without intent to repay; in declaring unjust, improper bankruptcies to avoid repayment of loans; in robbing on the street or in the home money and other precious possessions; in stealing time, giving less than a full day of honest labor for a full day's compensation; in riding public transportation without paying the fare; and all forms of dishonesty in all places and in all things. (November 1976, *Ensign,* 6)

We find ourselves in that "day of dishonor." For example, a 1999 issue of the *Ensign* features an essay by two Latter-day Saint social scientists whose research suggests that the youth of today's Church, although somewhat less culpable than American youth in general, are heavily involved in acts and attitudes of dishonesty. One wonders if this sad story reflects a fundamental immaturity among older members as well.

In writing to members of the Church just after the Savior's death, the apostle James warned: "A double-minded man is unstable in all his ways" (James 1:8). To be "double-minded" is to lack integrity. A double-minded person is one who says he is something he is not. A person can attend Church meetings, participate actively in a ward, and pretend to love others unselfishly, and yet be dishonest in his business dealings. A young man can be a seminary president and yet cheat on school tests. A Church member can take welfare aid and yet not follow the counsel of his priesthood leaders. A Brigham Young University student's education is more than half paid by sacred tithing funds, yet he may be lazy, or irreverent, or silly rather than sober, industrious, and consciously grateful. Children can be very quick to condemn unrighteousness and yet continue to associate with unrighteous persons, and even spend a great deal of time and effort making excuses for their loyalty to the unrighteous. A bishop can try his best to do all things with charity and forbearance and yet unconciously be more concerned with whether he is liked than that he holds to the Lord's standards. An active Latter-day Saint can stand for law and order and yet consistently break traffic laws by rolling through stop signs, speeding, and tail-gating, and then make light of it as if such misdemeanor behavior did not matter. When we do these things and have this cavalier dishonesty we shall be at war within ourselves, and also shall always have what seems to us perfectly good excuses for our behavior. A person with integrity, however, will be unified with a desire to serve God at all costs and to have total honesty regardless of the consequences, and he will not indulge in rationalization. He will be calm and at peace within himself.

In *Faith Precedes the Miracle*, President Kimball affirms that "no virtues in the perfection we strive for are more important than integrity and honesty: let us then be complete, unbroken, pure, and sincere, to develop in ourselves that quality of soul" (248). Total integrity would mean that words are not measured to make sure that only the technical truth is given, but that thoughts, emotions, ideas, and problems are truthfully shared and received in appropriate contexts. Total integrity would mean that parents would be very careful in what they promise a child, because a broken promise may have lasting consequences. Total integrity would mean that one would recognize lying as both giving false information and being silent about others doing it. Total integrity would mean that habits of self-justification would be recognized and discarded immediately.

II

Integrity is intimately connected to maturity. Integrity, from the Latin *integritas,* means wholeness, completeness, having no part missing. The processs of maturing, from the Latin *maturare*, means to come to a wholeness, to grow to a completeness of being. To say that a person has integrity is to say that he or she is a spiritually mature person. Of course, all of us are relatively spiritually immature compared to the Savior, because we are all in the process of maturing into a full measure of our creation (*Doctrine and Covenants* 1:10 and 88:19, 25). But it is impossible to be mature without integrity. Note the following ways in which are manifest differences between a spiritually mature person and a spiritually immature person, between a person with integrity and one riddled with moral flaws.

1. A spiritually immature person sins frequently and sometimes seriously (Helaman 4:11–13), whereas a spiritually mature person sins infrequently and less seriously (*Doctrine and Covenants* 58:42–43).

2. A spiritually immature person commits the same sin over and over again (*Doctrine and Covenants* 82:7), whereas a spiritually mature person repents and does not return to the sin.

3. The spiritually immature resist chastisement or refuse to be corrected (I Nephi 16:2), but the spiritually mature accept chastisement, especially from those in ecclesiastical or familial authority (II Timothy 3:16).

4. An immature person resists repentance or refuses to admit guilt, or does so slowly (Helaman 13:38), but a person of integrity repents as quickly as possible (*Doctrine and Covenants* 109:21).

5. Those without integrity and maturity blame others for their sins and misdeeds (*Doctrine and Covenants* 121:17), but the mature accept responsibility for their own sins (Moses 4:18).

6. Characteristic of spiritual immaturity is the attempt to cover up and gloss over sins (*Doctrine and Covenants* 121:37), but at the core of integrity is the fearlessness of recognizing personal weakness and confessing sins (*Doctrine and Covenants* 58:43).

7. A spiritually immature person thinks he or she cannot repent (Alma 30:17), but a spiritually mature person fully accepts the atonement of Jesus Christ (*Doctrine and Covenants* 76:51–53).

8. Spiritual immaturity and lack of integrity is manifest in a person's tendency to remain unrepentant while acting as though she or he is righteous (Romans 1:22), whereas maturity and integrity are shown in a willingness to suffer whatever it takes to confess and make full restitution for sins (Mosiah 3:19).

9. An immature person allows sin to paralyze action and inhibit progess (*Doctrine and Covenants* 121:34-35), but a spiritually mature person continues, and even tries harder, to do good and work on personal goals while repenting of sins (*Doctrine and Covenants* 124:113–114).

10. A spiritually immature and morally flawed person accuses others of hypocrisy and focuses on others' perceived faults (Jude 1:8, 10, 16), whereas a person of integrity concentrates on her or his own sins and supports those who are trying to do good and who openly stand against evil (III Nephi 13:14–15).

11. An immature person lacking in integrity engages in enabling behavior and calls the enabling behavior "love" (I Timothy 5:22), but a spiritually mature person does not enable others to continue in sin by making excuses for them, by being non-confrontive, by trying to "rescue," or by invoking "non-judgemental" attitudes and behaviors (*Doctirne and Covenants* 75:20).

12. A mark of immaturity and dishonesty is a refusal to judge at all (Moroni 7:15–16), but care to judge righteously is the sign of spiritual maturity (Matthew 7:1–2).

13. A spiritually immature person is unrealistic, living in the past or in a made-up world, whereas a spiritually mature person is realistic, and does not lie, pretend, shift focus, construe the past as present, or manipulate facts to fit feelings (II Corinthians 5:7).

14. An immature person is defensive and easily offended (Moroni 10:22), but a spiritually mature person accepts criticism as a way to grow (*Doctrine and Covenants* 122:2).

15. A spiritually immature person is self-centered (III Nephi 6:15–16), but a mature person is altruistic, service-oriented, and considerate of others within the principles of righteousness (I Corinthians 8:1).

16. Those lacking in integrity are impatient (*Doctrine and Covenants* 98:24), but the spiritually mature are patient in trials (Romans 5:3).

17. A spiritually immature person is light-minded (*Doctrine and Covenants* 59:15), but a spirtually mature person, while maintaining a sense of humor, is sober (Mosiah 4:15).

18. A spritually immature and worldly person has stronger feelings to biological and social than to covenant relationships, or equal feelings for all (doing a "balancing act" between the world's realtionships and those of the eternities), whereas a mature person has stronger instincts, feelings, and loyalties to covenant relationships and to those who keep covenants than to relationships with those who violate covenants (*Doctrine and Covenants* 25:13).

19. Spiritual immaturity is characterized by an inability to discern righteouness from unrighteousness (II Nephi 15:20), but integrity is marked by the ability to discern by the Spirit (*Doctrine and Covenants* 46:23).

20. Spiritual immaturity is marked by personal irresponsibility (that is, by making choices that have consequences negatively affecting others, or by making decisions without the personal resources to carry them out), but spiritual maturity is personal responsibility personified.

The prophets have said a surprisingly large number of things about spiritual maturity and integrity during the modern history of the Church. A number of things they have said recall a story President Kimball told:

> I stepped into a restaurant to buy something and a woman I knew was sitting at the counter with a cup of coffee at her plate. I am sure she saw me, although she tried not to show it. I could see her physical discomfort as she turned her face from me at a right angle. What a wallop her character had taken because of her action. How she shriveled! At the waters of baptism, in sacrament meetings, and in the temple, she had promised that she would have a broken heart and a contrite spirit, that she would repent of all her sins, that she would take upon herself the name of Jesus Christ, and serve him to the end, manifesting it by her works. The ten stories of the building above her were not enough to keep the angels in heaven from recording her movements and thoughts of deception. It was a petty thing, but a withering thing

> —a weak, mean, cheap, little tricky thing that sent her honor skidding downward toward the bankruptcy of self-esteem. (*Faith Precedes the Miracle*, 241–2)

Contrast this with two stories, both of them personal and precious.

My wife's paternal grandfather spent a lifetime of backbreaking work, raising sheep in order to make a living for his large family. In one season the herd was wiped out in a disaster not of his making. His "friends," if we can call them that, advised him to take out bankruptcy, and he would never have to pay back all his debts. But he refused, saying that he could not live with himself if he let someone else take care of his problem. His "friends" told him he was crazy not to take advantage of bankruptcy law. But he spent the rest of his life paying off his debts, little-by-little, until all was even. He had maintained his integrity rather than let bankruptcy laws "buy him off."

A neighbor of mine in the town where I grew up told me about a conversation in which he had engaged years before. The man with whom he was conversing was from out-of-state and knew little about small-town Westerners. "But I know of one," he said. "He is so honest that I trust him completely. If you are all like this man, I'd like to know what produces you." My neighbor then learned that the man was speaking of my father.

Now, in order to mature and to increase our integrity we must learn to be more sensitive to the details of everyday living, the places where our integrity really manifests itself. If we have deep problems that involve public dishonor to the Church, we need to confess to our priesthood leaders right now. In any case, it might be effective to fall to our knees without delay and thank Heavenly Father for his mercies, and ask him to quicken our minds and hearts in a deepening of our integrity and a forgiveness of times when we have been less than mature.

President Harold B. Lee posed a situation that summarizes what all this means.

> "When we pass through the portals of death...He's going to say to us, 'Now you took upon yourselves my name. What have you done with my name? Have you ever brought disgrace to the name of the Lord Jesus Christ...?' Imagine a frown, imagine He shakes His head and turns and walks away...But imagine when we meet Him that a smile lights up His face. He puts out His beckoning arms to us, and says to us, 'My son, my daughter, you've been faithful on earth. You've kept

the faith. You've finished your work. There's now a crown prepared for such as you in my kingdom...' I can't think of any ecstasy in all the world that will transcend that kind of a reception into the presence of the Almighty, in that world to come (*Teachings*, 228)."

Idea Two: STEWARDSHIP

Spiritual Wheatfields, Emotional Vineyards

Countless saints throughout the eternities testify that the holy priesthood has been restored through the prophet Joseph Smith, that its unbroken line of authority has moved through other prophets down to President Gordon B. Hinckley, and that it will continue to move on in an orderly fashion after him. Priesthood allows righteous dominion, a proper working stewardship for God's purposes. We have the unsurpassed opportunity to hold God-given priesthood stewardships.

I

The ancient psalmist sang "the earth is the Lord's, and the fullness thereof; the world, and they that dwell therein" (Psalms 24:11). In our own dispensation the Lord declares

> Verily I say, that inasmuch as ye do this, the fullness of the earth is yours, the beasts of the field and the fowls of the air, and that which climbeth upon the trees and walketh upon the earth; Yea, all things which come of the earth, in the season thereof, are made for the benefit and use of man, both to please the eye and gladden the heart; Yea, for food and for raiment, for taste and for smell, to strengthen the body and to enliven the soul. And it pleaseth God that he hath given all these things unto man; for unto this end were they made to be used, with judgment, not to excess, neither by extortion." (*Doctrine and Covenants* 59:16–20)

The point is that the earth itself was organized as a place where God's spirit children could, first of all, gain bodies of flesh and bone and, secondly, prove themselves in order to qualify for further progress (*Pearl of Great Price*, Abraham 3:22–26). The Book of Mormon calls this life a "probationary state."

Inasmuch as the earth is the Lord's, and He prepared it for our blessing, and this life is a probationary state for the development of God's children, we are all accountable to God in all things. In short, every person is a steward.

When the gospel was restored through Joseph Smith, and then during the early Kirtland period through the Nauvoo period, the Lord gave His prophet a number of particularly pointed revelations on the subject of stewardship. Interestingly, some of those revelations name stewardship as a law, the *defining relationship* between God and man, the agreement concerning which are called *covenants*. Note the importance of what the Lord has revealed about stewardship (*Doctrine and Covenants* 42, 51, 70, 72, 78) and observe how covenants and stewardship are two sides of the same coin. The principle or law of stewardship is binding upon us, and in appropriate measure upon every human being.

Many scriptural passages reveal that every person will be judged according to his or her own works (Matthew 16:27; Revelation 20:13; 1 Nephi 15:33; *Doctrine and Covenants* 19:3 1). Stewardship is a specific and precise formulation of the concept of individual responsibility, the same responsibility about which we make covenants. After relating the parable of the unjust steward, the Lord made the following declaration:

> He that is faithful in that which is least is faithful also in much: and he that is unjust in the least in unjust also in much. If therefore ye have

> not been faithful in the unrighteous mammon, who will commit to your trust the true riches? And if ye have not been faithful in that which is another man's, who shall give you that which is your own? (Luke 16:10–12)

Here are the three absolute and binding ideas about stewardship we learn from this:

> 1. If one cannot be faithful in a *small* stewardship he will never be entrusted with a *larger* one.
>
> 2. If one cannot responsibly use his *worldly* goods for righteous purposes he will never be entrusted with *eternal* dominion.
>
> 3. If one cannot ultimately be faithful in the care of the *Lord's* things he cannot expect to have his *own* things in the eternities.

Now, it could be argued that the most impressive statement the Lord made regarding the final judgment concerns the law of stewardship. He said that when the Son of Man comes in His glory He will separate men one from another "as a shepherd divideth his sheep from the goats." The basis of the division is the use one makes of what he has in rendering service to others. Those who are faithful in the use of what they have in rendering service to others are the "doers of the word," the faithful stewards, and will receive eternal life. On the contrary, those who are unfaithful, selfish, careless, and indifferent in the use of what they have, and do not render service commensurate with their ability, are the "non-doers of the word": the unfaithful stewards, the "goats," as it were. They will "go away into everlasting punishment" (Matthew 25:31–46). In our own day the Lord has reaffirmed the same principle with unequivocal force: "If any man shall take of the abundance which I have made, and impart not his portion, according to the law of my gospel, unto the poor and the needy, he shall, with the wicked, lift up his eyes in hell, being in torment" (*Doctrine and Covenants* 104:18). But instructions concerning the poor and needy are just one part of this law and warning: "And take heed to yourselves, lest at any time your hearts be overcharged with surfeiting (indulging), and drunkenness, and cares of this life, and so that day come upon you unawares. For as a snare shall it come on all them that dwell on the face of the whole earth" (Luke 21:34–5).

We are required to impart all we have in the care of our covenant stewardships or else our so-called "service" means nothing. When we are unfaithful, selfish, or indifferent to any degree in any covenant, we have failed our stewardship "test."

One of the most comprehensive statements the Lord has made about the law of stewardship is His wonderful parable of the ten pounds ("talents," or units of wealth). Here He speaks of a certain nobleman who was going into a far country to receive a kingdom for himself, and before leaving he called each of his ten servants and gave to each one pound. Upon receiving his kingdom he returned and asked his servants to give an account of what they had done with their respective stewardships. One servant had increased his pound to ten and was given authority over ten cities. Another servant had increased his pound to five and was given authority over five cities. A third servant had done nothing with his pound and offered a poor excuse for having done nothing; consequently, his pound was taken from him and given to him who had ten. In addition to the three categories of faithfulness (or the lack of it) here described, the parable also includes mention of citizens of the kingdom who rejected the nobleman as their king. When the servants gave their accounting, those who rejected the king were slain (Luke 19:11–28). These four categories suggest what Heavenly Father described to Joseph Smith in the vision of the three degrees of glory. That is, all those who are valiant and faithful in their stewardships will be heirs of the celestial kingdom of glory. Those who are good but less valiant and faithful to their stewardships will be heirs of the terrestrial glory. Those who are not valiant at all to their stewardships will lose them, but will eventually be heirs of the telestial glory. And those citizens of the kingdom who rebel against the Lord (that is, leave their covenants) will be condemned to perdition (see *Doctrine and Covenants* 76).

It is wise to remember that everyone has a stewardship. Every stewardship requires the same amount of time, talent, and energy; namely, all the time, talent, and energy a person has. This is as true for the local ward "hymnbook picker-upper" as it is for the prophet, as true for the single person as it is for the husband and wife with ten children. *The Lord does not discriminate on the basis of what we have, but on the basis of what we do with what we have.* Heavenly Father has said: "For it is expedient that I, the Lord, should make every man accountable, as a steward over earthly blessings, which I have made and prepared for my creatures"

(*Doctrine and Covenants* 104:13). Furthermore, eventually we will have to give an accounting of our stewardships to our priesthood leader, ecclesiastically for our Church callings, or patriarchially for our family callings (see Bruce R. McConkie, *Doctrines of Salvation: Sermons and Writings of Joseph Fielding Smith*, 111, 117). Every person who has received the covenant of baptism has the responsibility to be faithful to his stewardship irrespective of the type of calling he has in the Church. Every person who has received the sealing covenant in the temple has the responsibility to be faithful to his covenants irrespective of the special circumstances of family he may face. The consequences for the violation of these covenants will come as readily and as surely upon the "ordinary" member of the Church as it will upon an apostle: anyone who turns away into forbidden paths and neglects his duty has failed his stewardship "test."

II

Here are four suggestions about how to better take care of our stewardships. First of all, remember *four factors* that determine how any responsibility, whether great or small, can be handled. These factors are time, talent, means, and opportunity. Every individual is a custodian of these four factors. Each individual must realize that his of her authority to act is commensurate with his or her stewardship and the thoroughness with which that stewardship is handled. "And whoso is found a faithful, a just, and a wise steward shall enter into the joy of the Lord, and shall inherit eternal life" (*Doctrine and Covenants* 51:19): this promise is founded upon how we use these four factors.

Second, *get all the way into covenants and their implications.* We know for example that a worthwhile church leader is responsible to see that every church member under his charge qualifies for the celestial kingdom. And we have often heard from the pulpit that the depth of our commitment is measured by the quality of our performance. It is clear that obedience is the mark of commitment. This is how stewardship works: the "test" of whether or not we are faithful stewards is whether or not we provide service and devotion to every aspect of the commitment and every implication of the commitment. This is true of all stewardships, whether a Church calling, a parental role, or (and especially) a marriage.

Third, *remember human nature.* People are very complex beings. A man or woman is a composite of many different emotions, experiences, attitudes, prejudices, needs, and roles. One person may be a fisherman, garage mechanic, elders quorum president, father, club member, piano player, student, and husband all at the same time. Another person may be a mother, school teacher, stake young women's president, quilt-maker, violinist, and wife all at the same time. Each makes certain demands that may tend to pull the person in different directions, so the righteous will make certain that priorities are straight and responsible behavior is present. Added to the complexity of who a person is, is the problem of who a person thinks he is. All of us have some sort of self-image. The way we think about ourselves, the things we believe about ourselves, all go to form our self-image. Our self-image usually determines our behavior. If a teen-age girl pictures herself as a spiritual daughter of our Father in Heaven and a worthwhile, intelligent, well-thought-of, spiritual person, she will very likely behave in a commensurate way. It is difficult, perhaps impossible, for a young man to commit a grievous sin if he sees himself as a sparkling, physically pure son of God.

Everyone has some very deep responsibilities pertaining to the destiny of those in his or her stewardship. We are often the strongest influence in someone else's life. As we work in and supervise our dominions, we have the privilege of helping others discover their true worth, and this is the most thrilling reward there is. But as we seek to help we will encounter problems, usually where a person's self-image results in behavior that protects his or her self-opinion. We often may be confronted with conduct that is really an attempt to protect one's self-image, especially two behaviors: rationalizing and aggressiveness. Rationalizing (excusing, justifying, or scapegoating unacceptable behavior) is rampant. We have all heard such things as "I cannot come to the meeting because I have too much to do to get ready for work tomorrow," or "I do not want to get a certificate of achievement—what does a silly piece of paper mean, anyway?" or "I know he does not live the commandments, but I feel like I owe him at least some of my respect and time, and, anyway, he is one of God's children too," or "If the Bishop were just more understanding of my circumstances I could go along with what he is saying," etc. Aggressiveness (striking out in hostility, bitterness, belittling, meanness disguised as humor, aggressive passivity [stalling, refusing, forgetting]) is just as rampant. Weak people will strike out against that which threatens their self-image and makes them feel insecure. And righteousness is very intimidating to the weak.

Fourth, *fix attention.* A study of the lives of people of great accomplishment reveals that most had the ability to totally rivet their attention on what they were trying to accomplish. We need to have this kind of fierce determination in order to properly live in covenants and handle our stewardships. Husbands and wives need to be constantly attentive to their covenants and to one another, with total attention fixed on their commitments and the implications of those commitments, rather than on their self-images. An elders quorum president must be totally determined that home teaching, for example, is going to be done, no matter how much it may cost him, and fix his attention on how to accomplish the task prioritized within his other covenant commitments.

It seems clear that we must keep this in mind: *stewardship is about commitment and service.* One could say that stewardship is "responsible service," or service organized by covenants. Service is charity, and charity is giving. My wise grandfather taught that "there are only two kinds of people in the world; 'givers' and 'takers.'" We are not likely to trust or follow a "taker"—we are only likely to trust a "giver."

An interesting way to analogize the essence of stewardship and service is to think of Palestine's geography. There are two seas there, one fresh and the other salty. People drink from the waters of the first but avoid the second. The Jordan River makes these seas by bringing a constant flow of good water into them, and yet there is a profound difference between these neighboring bodies. Although the river pours the same good water into both, the Sea of Galilee receives but does not keep it. Water comes into this sea and water flows out again. But the Dead Sea receives water and lets none of it go.

There are two kinds of people in the world. The first impulse of the one is to give. The first impulse of the other is to take. One is sweet stewardship. The other is indulgent irresponsibility.

Idea Three: ADVERSITY

Barbed Wire and Dandelions

There are some today who would resent the natural workings of life in all its complexity, its trials, and its tribulations. Of course, no "normal" person will seek after adversity. But consider this: no spiritual person will seek to nullify the nature of and reason for mortal experience. President Howard W. Hunter wisely points out that

> Friction, or resistance, is an interesting phenomenon. Without this force, a person or vehicle could not move about or, if already in motion, could not be stopped except by collision. Simple things like nails, screws, and bolts would not stay in place; a cork would not stay in a bottle; a light globe would drop from its socket; a lid would not stay on a jar. (*That We Might Have Joy* 98)

In short, it is necessary for us to understand that if we walk off a cliff, we fall. It makes no difference whether we know the cliff is there, or whether we know we will fall if we walk off, or whether we want to fall, or whether we step off the cliff gently or take a long run at it, whether we fall five feet or five hundred feet, or whether someone pushes us off and it isn't our fault. The result is inevitable. It is in the nature of the thing. Our ignorance, our preferences, our carelessness, our culpability—all are irrelevant to cliffs and gravity. There are immutable results that come from natural law; they execute themselves; they do not depend upon our knowledge, our consent, or our desires. Life, like cliffs and gravity, is the way it is, and we cannot pretend it is different than it is. That is, when we fall off cliffs, or are pushed off cliffs, gravity will take over. When we hit bottom it hurts, and that is just the way it is.

Many have suffered heart-ripping and gut-twisting trials in life, and at times those who suffer adversity ask questions like, "Why me?" "Why would God allow such a tragedy?" "How can I bear up under this burden of care and worry and sorrow? "What did I do to deserve this?" To sufferers of adversity who ask questions like these I offer two fundamental thoughts in reply: (1) We must understand that adversity comes even to the righteous, and (2) We must understand that adversity has a purpose.

I

Adversity is in the nature of things. We do not always know why bad things happen to us or to others, and we do not need to know. Problems we face are not always the result of our own sins and weaknesses, and do not always come by way of the Lord's punishment. Too, we often suffer adversity because we get implicated in the evil decisions of others. Job finally recognized the nature of things when he declared that "man is born for trouble, even as the sparks (of a fire) fly upward." The point is: reality is so complicated that we do not know the causes and effects of things, and it is counterproductive (and even dangerous) to try to attribute bad effects to definite causes. Only under the influence of the Holy Spirit can we know the connections—but usually we do not need to know those connections.

Adversity and righteousness are connected. Let us think about righteousness for a moment. Remember that "righteousness" is not Christ-like righteousness if it is self-interested. Satan understands this fact very well and manipulates our misunderstanding of it. When the Adversary (the original adversity) stands in the presence of the Lord in the opening of The Book of Job he replies to the Lord's inquiry about Job in telling and cutting words; "Doth Job fear God for naught?" God had asked Satan if he knew Job and his righteousness. Satan said that indeed he did, but was not impressed. You see, every time Job had been righteous God had given him a blessing. That had shown only that Job was smart enough to operate in his own self-interest. Satan knows that anyone will do that: indeed, that is exactly how Satan himself operates. Such behavior is only selfishness, not righteousness. So God takes away Job's blessings in order to see if Job will be righteous just for the sake of righteousness instead of for the sake of getting a blessing. The question for us is the same: do we obey the commandments for gain? Or do we obey the commandments just because it is right to do so? Until we get the difference between these two approaches clear in our minds and hearts we will never understand the connection between adversity and righteousness.

Adversity brings out the worst in us: indeed, that is the point. We cannot make progress until we face who we really are with all our spiritual blemishes and flaws. Tribulations tend to strip away the fondly-held lies we hold about ourselves; trials knock from our faces the rose-colored glasses with which we view our own "wonderful" qualities. Forced into a clearer view of ourselves, we have the opportunity to see clearly how much we must rely on the Lord. Perhaps even more important is the opportunity we have, under the scouring surge of adversity, to see the magnificence of the Lord in His perfections and to catch the chasm that lies between His godliness and our imperfection. We sometimes come a little late to the obvious conclusion that without being in the depths of our humility we cannot approach the Lord.

Adversity shows us that things could be worse. This is a simple but profound fact of life that only gets obscured when in our arrogance we believe we have the right to feel sorry for ourselves. There is always someone worse off than we are. And it is always possible for things to be worse for us than they are at the moment. Remember the Lord's plan: all things being equal in our attempts to be good people, Heavenly Father will not allow our circumstances to be greater than we can bear. Things could be greater than we could bear, but they aren't that bad because of the Lord's mercy.

The 121st section of the *Doctrine and Covenants* suggests that the purpose for the trials and tribulations the prophet Joseph Smith endured was so that he could be refined enough to receive revelation and help bring about the Lord's purposes. We are, in our own way, in an analogous situation. Adversity can refine us spiritually (and sometimes emotionally and physically too), thus putting us on a new plane of reference, a higher level of performance, the view from which gives us a way to be an ever greater instrument in Heavenly Father's hands.

II

Life is so ordered that adversity will come. When it does come, how shall we handle it? How can we make the most of adversity? Adversity is like barbed wire. View these images for a moment (Peer, 37):

The Barbed-Wire Fence

Pocked posts, enclosing ditches
Of shifting sand, sun-seared heat on dry grass.
Walking this line, sleepless, in fever;
No way around, through, under,
Or out.

Nothing of dreaming new dimensions,
Of lines breaking and haunting the horizon.
Hooked into skin, sliced down hands,
Run head-on against this blind wall,
Right in.
Caught clean a dappled yellow-brown paper,
Perhaps a random, wind-blown notice
Of our cuts, sweating fevers, punctured flesh,
And anger. The last barb in that paper eye blinds
So that we see in and out of boundaries
And fence-lines.

If we persist in running head-long into barbed wire, and if we are angry that the fence is in our way, we shall surely be cut and torn. But if we regard the barbed-wire fences of our experience as lines of defense, as protective barriers against going over into a place we do not belong (or that is too dangerous for us) then we may come to understand the need for fences, even barbed-wire ones.

Here are a few "don'ts" for adversity:

1. Don't panic. Just as certainly as trials come, they go away.

2. Don't feel sorry for yourself. It could be worse and it *is* worse for many.

3. Don't seek a scapegoat. Just take responsibility for dealing with hurts and trials without trying to make yourself feel better by pretending that deflecting helps. Remember: deflection defeats you.

4. Don't react with anger and disappointment. These emotions canker the spirit and, worse, create problems for others.

Adversity is like dandelions. One of the most beautiful moments I have ever spent was in a high mountain meadow in the Austrian Alps one summer day. This meadow was full of blooming edelweiss, alpine honeysuckle, and huge dandelions interspersed wildly within grasses of different varieties and shades of green and purple. The wind moved across the face of this meadow almost imperceptibly, lifting aromas into the air. The wild variety of those plants and smells remain forceful in my mind and heart to this day. Such a kind of beauty and wonder I have seldom experienced in such a heightened way. Now, back home we spend great effort trying to kill the dandelions in our lawns. But, you see, we only hate dandelions and try to get rid of them if we want a lawn instead of a meadow. We only hate adversity and battle against it ever touching our lives if we want a closely clipped and trimmed front-yard spirituality rather than a freely-growing, never-to-be-forgotten, high-mountain spirituality.

Now here are a few "do's" for aversity:

1. Do respond with submissiveness. We may be momentarily disheartened, but we must remember that life is the way it is and is not meant to

be easy. Trials must be borne and grief endured with humility along the way. Elder Russell M. Nelson (*Ensign*, May 1988) has pointed out that we cannot foster our faith without submissiveness, for only upon conditions of our submissiveness will the Lord give us power and protection. If we meet adversity with dignity and submissiveness we have the Lord's promise: "I will be on your right hand and on your left, and my Spirit shall be in your hearts, and mine angels round about you, to bear you up" (*Doctrine and Covenants* 84:88).

2. Do step back and ask "what can I learn from this?" The Lord often chooses to instruct His people in their times of trial. Church history and the Scriptures show that some of Heavenly Father's most lasting lessons have been taught through the trials and tribulations we all face. This does not mean that the Lord creates the adversities, but that He uses the adversity that comes to us to teach us that which we would not understand were we not suffering.

3. Do remember that in the pre-mortal existence we knew there was going to be adversity *and we agreed to it.* President Marion G. Romney said it best (*Conference Report*, October 1969): "We all knew when we elected to come into mortality, that we would here be proved in the crucible of adversity and affliction."

4. Do overcome trials by exercising patience. Elder Richard G. Scott suggests that the teachings of the Savior are the key to meeting tribulation with patience (*Ensign*, November 1991) : "(The teachings of Jesus Christ) emphasize that it matters very much what we ask for and how we ask for it. Blessings come when we ask the Father in the name of Christ, diligently keep His commandments, ask with faith in Christ, ask for that which is right, harden not our hearts, (and) express gratitude."

Since help from the Lord usually comes in increments, it would be foolish for us to fail to endure until help and healing is complete. Once a relative asked President Spencer W. Kimball for a blessing to combat a crippling disease. For some time President Kimball prepared himself spiritually; then, fasting, he was prompted to bless her to be healed. Some weeks later she returned, angry and complaining that she was fed up with waiting for the Lord to give the promised relief. He responded that he now understood why she had not been blessed. One must be patient, do one's part, and express gratitude for the smallest improvement noted. She repented, followed his counsel, and eventually was made well.

Let us remember this: it is not *that* we suffer adversity, but *what we do about it* that is the point of mortality. In fact, the instant we get this point clear in our minds and hearts, the instant the Holy Ghost will be able to bless our lives in new ways. Heavenly Father knows us perfectly, He knows what we can bear, He is not fooled by our egocentrism, and He has His purposes. He does not necessarily cause our adversities, but when we do suffer (just because we live in this complex interpenetration of a reality) He will be at our side. Will we see Him there? It is imperative to focus not so much on the elimination of pain but on having the heart to endure it to the end so that the Lord's purposes for us may be fulfilled.

Idea Four: PRAYER

The Soul's Sincere Desire

Jesus taught very plainly what we must do if we are to be happy, productive, of service to others, and clear on what is right: "Ye must always pray unto the Father in my name" (3 Nephi 18:19). One of the great exemplars of prayer is, of course, Joseph Smith who, "in the midst of this war of words and tumult of opinions" and asking himself what could possibly be done about happiness and truth, read in James 1:5 "If any of you lack wisdom, let him ask of God..." (*History of the Church*, 1:4–6). His prayer was answered, he did the Lord's bidding, and through his influence the world changed so much that it can never be the same again.

I

Prayer is a sincere desire to have a heartfelt and guileless talk with Heavenly Father, followed by actually talking to Him. We pray to Heavenly Father and to no one else, to no other being or to no object or creation (Exodus 20:3-5). We pray in the name of Jesus Christ, since he is our intermediary, but we pray directly to our Heavenly Father. Communication with deity requires the highest respect, by definition, so we always use authorized prayer language in whatever language is our native tongue. In English we use "thou," "thee," "thy," and "thine" rather than "you," "your," and "yours." It could be regarded as disrespectful deliberately to fail to use prayer language. The use of prayer language is not a personal choice; it is required by God. No matter where we are, no matter whether we are kneeling in private or standing in public, no matter whether we speak out loud in our private prayers or silently as appropriate, no matter whether we are praying by ourselves or as spokesman for a group, we must always pray with respect, as Moroni says, "with a sincere heart, with real intent" (Moroni 10:4).

As we pray to our Heavenly Father we tell Him what we really feel in our hearts and really think in our minds. We must confide in Him, plead with Him, thank Him with all our hearts and minds. Meaningless words and phrases are blasphemous, and overused, clichéd phraseology shows a lack of thoughtful, concentrated effort on our part to really communicate. Lazy language is not part of true prayer. When young people pray, it is well to think about exactly what you are saying, and avoid silliness and the mere repetition of somebody else's way of saying something. When parents teach children how to pray, it is important to help them say what they really think and feel in their language, not what a memorized list of prayer phrases shapes them to say. When more mature people pray, it might help to avoid the superficial sentimentality that throws stickiness into the wheels of communication and hopelessly stalls the kind of mature sincerity God expects of us. We thank and request, we plead and apologize, we seek and we find; but we must always ask that His will be done, remembering that we may not always know exactly what may be best for us (3 Nephi 18:20).

We may wonder when to pray. Heavenly Father has asked us to pray privately at least each morning and night (Alma 34:21). We are counseled to have regular family prayer each morning and night. We have the privilege of praying to give thanks and ask a blessing on our food before each time we eat anything. We open and close all official Church meetings with prayer.

We might well ask, "what is prayer for, anyway?" The Bible, Book of Mormon, Doctrine and Covenants, and Pearl of Great Price as well as the words of the prophets give us some ideas. Basically, prayer is to be used as the binding element in all the things we do in order to obtain that which cannot be obtained in any other way. So we pray in order to get closer to Heavenly Father. We pray to increase our knowledge. We pray to resist evil and temptation. We pray to increase our strength of character. Even more fundamentally, prayer is the key to spiritual maturity. I think of the sermon of the prophet Moroni:

> And now my brethren, I judge these things of you because of your peaceable walk with the children of men. For I remember the word of God, which saith by their works ye shall know them; for if their works be good, then they are good also. For behold, God hath said a man being evil cannot do that which is good; for if he offereth a gift, or prayeth unto God, except he shall do it with real intent it profiteth him nothing. For behold, it is not counted unto him for righteousness. For behold, if a man being evil giveth a gift, he doeth it grudgingly; wherefore it is counted unto him the same as if he had retained the gift; wherefore he is counted evil before God. And likewise also it is counted evil unto a man, if he shall pray and not with real intent of heart; yea, and it profiteth him nothing, for God receiveth none such. (Moroni 7:4–9).

In an *Improvement Era* article President Joseph F. Smith calls this Book of Mormon passage "applicable to far too many Latter-day Saints." He says:

> ...one of the greatest follies I have ever witnessed is the foolish custom of...repeating...prayer continually without considering its meaning... It thus becomes only a form; there is no power in it, neither is it acceptable because it is not offered from the heart nor with the understanding... It is desirable for us to look well to our words when we call upon the Lord... What we need...for our own good, is to go before Him often, to witness unto Him that we remember Him and that we are willing to...keep His commandments [and] work righteousness.

> [Let all prayers] come from the heart, let [them] not be in words that are worn into ruts in the beaten tracks of common use...

President Smith continues, referring to the link between prayer and the commandment God has given each of us to judge behavior, events, consequences, and attitudes:

> ...if we as Latter-day Saints, believing as we do in the divinity (of the scriptures and the words of the brethren), we would believe as children believe, with understanding, in faith, being sure that God inspired them, and then put them into practice [with prayer]. I think it would not be long before we could do away with [disciplinary councils] and with the present necessity for...visits to try to settle difficulties among Latter-day Saints. [Every man] would judge righteously, because he would judge in the light of Christ, in the light of truth, in the light of justice—not selfishly, not covetously, but in the light that [comes] from [heaven through revelation and prayer]. (August, 1908; 11:729–32)

We need not willy-nilly subscribe to the world's value-subjective and relativistic dictum to neither judge nor be judgmental, but through study and prayer, insight and compassion, following Gospel principles and more prayer, learn to judge correctly and righteously. Prayer is the key.

II

And we shall know if our prayer is truly sincere if, as we pray for help, we do all within our power to bring about that for which we pray. We may have felt at times that no matter how long and hard we have prayed, and no matter how hard you tried to put into action that for which you were praying, that your prayers remained unanswered. This is simply not possible. We have been clearly taught that "sincere prayers are always answered" (*Gospel Principles*, 43). Sometimes the answer to our prayer is "yes." Sometimes the answer is "no," because what we have asked for is not precisely best for us. Sometimes the answer is "wait a while for a 'yes' or 'no.'" Sometimes the answer is "make your own choice by your own best judgement." Our prayers are always answered *at a time* and *in a way* that Heavenly Father knows will help us most. And at times He may wait for us to ask the right question so that He can give us the answer He needs us to receive.

President Harold B. Lee recounted the following incident :

> We had a very grievous case that had to come before the High Council and the Stake Presidency which resulted in the excommunication of a man of a family who had a harmed a lovely young girl. After nearly an all-night session which resulted in this action, I went to my office rather weary the next morning to be confronted by a brother of this man whom we had had on trial the night before. This man said, "I want to tell you that my brother wasn't guilty of that thing which you charged him with." "How do you know he wasn't guilty?' I asked. "Because I prayed, and the Lord told me he was innocent," the man answered. I asked him to come into the office and we sat down, and I asked, "Would you mind if I asked you a few personal questions?" He said, "Certainly not." "How old are you?" "Forty-seven." "What Priesthood do you hold?" He said he thought he was a teacher. "Do you keep the Word of Wisdom?" and he said, "Well, no." He used tobacco, which was obvious. "Do you pay your tithing?" He said "No, and I don't intend to as long as that blankety- blank-blank man was the Bishop of the thirty-second ward." I said, "Do you attend your Priesthood meetings?" He replied that he did not and didn't intend to as long as that man was Bishop. "You don't attend your sacrament meetings either?" "No, sir." "Do you have your family prayers?" and he said no. "Do you study the scriptures?" He said well, his eyes were bad and he couldn't read very much. I then said to him: "in my home I have a beautiful instrument called a radio. When everything is in good working order we can dial it to a certain station and pick up a speaker or the voice of a singer all the way across the continent or sometimes on the other side of the world, bringing them into the front room as though they were almost speaking there. But after we had used it for a long time, there were some little delicate instruments or electrical devices on the inside called radio tubes that begin to wear out. When one of them wears out, we get a kind of static—it isn't so clear. Another wears out, and if we don't give it attention and another one wears out—well, the radio sits there looking quite like it did before, but something has happened on the inside. We can't get any singer. We can't get any speaker. Now," I said, "you and I have within our souls something like what might be said to be a counterpart of

> those radio tubes. We might have what we call a 'Go-to-Sacrament-Meeting-Tube,' a 'Keep-the-Word-of-Wisdom-Tube,' a 'Pay-Your-Tithing-Tube,' a 'Have-Your-Family-Prayers-Tube,' a 'Read-the-Scriptures-Tube,' and as one of the most important, the master tube of the whole soul, the 'Keep-Yourself-Morally-Clean-Tube.' If one of these becomes worn out by disuse or it is not active...it has the same effect upon our spiritual selves that that same worn out instrument in the radio in my home has upon the reception that we otherwise could receive... Now then," I said, "fifteen of the best men in the Pioneer Stake prayed last night. They heard the evidence and every man was united (in the judgement that) your brother was guilty. Now, you, who do none of these things, you say you prayed, and you got an opposite answer. How would you explain that?" Then the man gave an answer that I think was a classic. He said, "Well, President Lee, I think I must have gotten my answer from the wrong source." And you know that's just as great a truth as we can have. We get our answer from the source of power we list to obey. If we're keeping the commandments of (Satan), we'll get the answer from (Satan). If we're keeping the commandments of God, we'll get (answers) from our Heavenly Father for our direction and our guidance. (Speeches of the Year, BYU Press, 1952:4–6)

The being to whom we pray is actually the being who is the author of the behavioral patterns we follow. We know our intent is not pure and our prayers are not sincere if we fail to follow with exactness what our Priesthood leaders counsel us to do, because they follow Heavenly Father. And saying that they do not follow Heavenly Father, or do not really understand our problems, or that our answers to prayers are different than theirs, makes up one of Satan's basic behavioral patterns.

Remember that we can always find the truth and know how to judge and what to decide. First we must study our problem or the situation out completely. This means that we have to consult all sources and think them through very carefully. "All sources" means everything that the Lord has already revealed about the problem or situation in the Scriptures, the words of wise experts, and especially in all the words of ancient and modern prophets. When we have done this, no matter how much effort or how long it takes, then we are ready to take our problem to Heavenly Father in prayer.

Most issues we face are easy to solve: the answers have already been revealed. But those that are very particular to us and require Solomon-like judgement will require sincere and thoughtful prayer, the kind President Hinckley is reported to give. Bishop Robert D. Hales says that President Hinckley solves most problems by good judgement and long study, but "when he comes up against an insoluble problem, he goes to his knees" (Sheri L. Dew, *Gordon B. Hinckley—Go Forward With Faith*, 444). And sooner or later he always receives the answer he needs.

Heavenly Father not only listens to our prayers but also *always* gives us an answer either sooner or later. When our prayers are given in humility and obedience, they have mighty power.

Idea Five: COVENANTS

The New and Everlasting Categorical Imperative

The fullness of the Gospel is called by Heavenly Father the New and Everlasting Covenant. It is the master covenant of mortality, and includes constituent covenants made upon entry into the Kingdom (Baptism and Confirmation), at conferral of the Priesthood (Oath and Covenant of the Priesthood), in the Temple (Temple Endowment and Eternal Marriage), during Sacrament meeting (Sacrament of the Lord's Supper), and so on. Heavenly Father calls the master covenant "everlasting" because it is set in place by an everlasting God and because the covenant will never be taken away. The Lord gave this same covenant to Adam, Enoch, Noah, Abraham, and other prophets. In this sense it is not new but, according to Jeremiah 31 (13–34), Heavenly Father calls it "new" because each time the Gospel is restored after being taken from the earth, it is new to the people who receive it.

When we accept this master covenant and the constituent parts of it we agree to live by faith in the Lord Jesus Christ, to continually repent, to listen to the promptings of the Holy Ghost, and to live righteously to the end of our mortal probation. We must keep all constituent covenants of the master covenant with exactness. If we do, Heavenly Father says He will grant us "an exaltation in the celestial kingdom" (*Doctrine and Covenants* 1:32).

I

Many have said that we live in the most dangerous time in human history, a time in which there are more pressures more powerfully put to leave our covenants (or not to make them in the first place) than ever before. This assertion bears repeating: we live in the most dangerous time in history. Satan and his agents are putting more pressure on us to leave our covenants than ever before.

If we understand just what a covenant is, we do not fall prey to the Adversary's tricks of misdefinition. A covenant is an oath and a promise made "without conditions." Every covenant is a sacrament (the word "sacrament" comes from the Latin *sacramentum*, meaning "verbal oath") and is formalized by language addressed to the Lord. For example, the Sacrament of the Lord's supper is pronounced by the Priesthood officiators at the sacrament table. That prayer is the sacrament, the oath. Partaking of the bread and water is a witness that the sacrament was heard, understood, agreed with, and said "amen" to. In addition to being an oath, a covenant is a promise. Promises are not agreements made: they are assurances given. "Made with no conditions" means that we covenant without regard to others' perceptions, without making excuses, and without playing games with the Lord.

It would be wise to remember that, strictly speaking, *a covenant is not a contract.* A contract codifies a situation in which two parties "cut a deal" with each other ("I'll do this if you'll do that"). We do not cut deals with the Lord. A covenant is a promise to Heavenly Father to do and be certain things without regard to what the other party (the Lord) may do. The Lord will do what He will do: our only business is to do what we are supposed to do. Although the humble and diligent covenant-keeper has the right to supplicate the throne of mercy, such supplication is not done in the spirit of the wheeler-dealer. It is difficult to imagine anything more arrogant and shameful than for a mere mortal to believe he or she has a right to "cut a deal" with the Lord.

The distinction between a covenant and a contract could be outlined this way:

Contract	**Covenant**
•the parties to the agreement are equal	•the parties to the agreement are NOT equal
•the terms of the agreement are negotiable	•the terms of the agreement are NOT negotiable
•the agreement can be terminated at will (there can be an "out" clause)	•the agreement CANNOT be terminated at will (there is no "out" clause)
•the agreement is valid in this life	•the agreement is valid for eternity
•violation of the agreement possibly brings consequences	•violation of the agreement automatically brings penalties
•the agreement is made by striking a bargain	•the agreement is not struck by "bargaining" or "making deals"
•the agreement has a time limit	•the agreement has no time limit
•the agreement is entered into by signature or the like	•the agreement is entered into by eternal oath

A careful consideration of these differences reveals fundamental truths about covenants; namely that, first of all, they are under God's direction and control, not subject to human whim or manipulation; secondly, that they are everlasting rather than time-bound; and thirdly, that they are powerful rather than superficial. Covenants have the power and scope to bring everlasting joy, whereas contracts can bring only the possibility of a happiness that must inevitably come to an end.

Perhaps most importantly, it is wise to understand with deep soberness how much pain and sorrow, both for the covenant-maker and those associated with her/him, comes when a covenant is treated as though it were merely a contract.

Too, *a covenant is not a hypothesis.* A hypothesis expresses a situation in which an agreement may be supported by evidence one day and destroyed by it the next. A covenant is a promise to Heavenly Father to do and be certain things without looking for evidence supporting reasons for or against the promise and its consequences.

The point is that when we get all the way into the covenant we do not try to "cut deals" with the Lord and we do not treat our promises as hypotheses to be supported by Him. True covenant-makers joyfully agree to do and be certain things no matter what, realizing that their lot is cast without possibility of change.

Sadly there are those who do not remain in their covenants. This happens because they do not repent of their sins. In fact, most of us who are not all the way into our covenants, or who have pretended that for some reason our covenants no longer apply, are simply too proud to repent. Consider for a moment what repentance actually is.

II

The pains of repentance are in themselves very much like the pains of damnation. The sole difference between these moments of agony is in the attitude of the sufferers. All truly covenant people have grasped the great essential which is so often overlooked in arguments about how people change; namely, the prime necessity of accepting responsibility. That is why if a person is once convinced of his own guilt all punishment of whatever kind purges. Obviously, whether or not pain and punishment is remedial depends upon the will of the sufferer to make it so. If a guilty person is not convinced of her own guilt, then any punishment seems vindictive since she sees it as "unfair." The burning fire is just God's warmth as experienced by those who reject it. To those who cling to their sins, the burning reality of holiness is painful. To the repentant, punishment and pain is welcomed as a sick man welcomes the pains of surgery, in order that the crippling cancers of pride and defiance may be excised. The whole point of repentance and the pain that comes with it is the freeing of the self, for the unrepentant are imprisoned in the torture of having set themselves in defiance of Heavenly Father. Repentance is the relentless breaking-down, at whatever cost, of these prison walls, so that the spirit may emerge at last into liberty, so as to endure unscathed the unveiled light of divine reality. Keeping our covenants means to be constantly repentant so as to be free in God's presence.

Remember that the eternities are about getting what you want. Every one of us will get *exactly* what we really desire. If we insist on having our own way, we will get it: anything less than the celestial kingdom is simply the enjoyment of our own way forever. If we really want God's way for us, we will get it within our covenants in the celestial kingdom, and the pain, agony, sweat, tears, and shame of repentance will not deter us: they will be welcomed as the means to the ends of the covenant relationship.

We must remember that human beings are responsible. The sick notion that we are helpless puppets of circumstance, heredity, temperament, or environment, and therefore not liable for our thoughts and actions, is one which the prophets over and over again go out of their way to refute. That is why so many sermons from the pulpit deal with human agency. When every allowance is made, when mercy and pity and grace have done all they can, the consequences of sin are the sinner's, and he may face it in a spirit of sullen rebellion or of ready joy.

The contrast between those who are all the way into their covenants and those who are not is, therefore, in its essentials, a contrast of spiritual attitude. When we are all the way into the covenant, then no matter what it might cost us, we are repentant. In the simplest terms, this is what repentance is all about (see Dorothy L. Sayers discussion in *Introductory Papers,* 79 ff.). Suppose that, in anger, or through carelessness, you have damaged a valuable book belonging to a friend. The effect of this act is to disturb the relationship between you and in order to bring matters back to harmony it is necessary that you should, first of all, be sorry, and secondly, be forgiven.

If we look at this a little more closely, we see that the first necessity of repentance is that you should accept judgement; that is, you have to admit that you did wrong. The book did not just come to pieces in your hands, nobody knocked it out of your hands, nobody forced you to pick it up in the first place. Only your own ill-temper or your negligence is to blame. Notice that it also does not matter what your motive was: the fact is that the book is ruined. When you have frankly admitted, to yourself first and then to your friend, that the book is ruined, you have done the first thing in repentance: *open admission.* The next requirement is that you should be sorry that the book is ruined, that you say you are sorry that it is ruined, and that you say you are sorry for whatever it is in you that led to the book being ruined. Then you must ask to be forgiven. This second part of repentance is called *contrition.* When this is done your friend forgives you and good relations are restored. You are now, without any further act, free of the guilt of your act.

Two things, however, remain. First of all, the book is still ruined. Secondly, you are still liable to whatever caused you to ruin the book in the first place: that is, you just might ruin another book tomorrow. Therefore, you have yet to complete repentance. Of course, if you are sincere rather than a faker, you will want to do something about the damaged property. Even though you have been forgiven, you will want to make it up to your friend. Now the ruined books of our lives require more effort than we might suppose, because we can never restore the book to precisely the way it was. We can repair it, replace it with another, substitute something of even higher value than the original: but whatever we do, the original book will never be exactly the same. When we realize this, we are reduced to the most abject humility. We are powerless. This is why we have the atonement. The atonement restores the ruined books of our lives to their original pre-sin condition, something that is entirely impossible for us to do. And then we must rid ourselves of the tendency to fall into the same fault again. In other words, we must rid ourselves of any possibility that we might be ill-tempered or negligent in anything again. When we have done this, our repentance is complete.

Until our repentance is complete, we shall only be partly in our covenants. Indeed, the daily joyful struggle to repent is one of the basic things we covenant to do, as well as the prerequisite for honest keeping of the various aspects of the covenant itself.

III

Sadly, not everyone who has made sacred covenants keeps them. The Lord says:

> And as the covenant which they made unto me has been broken, even so it has become void and of none effect. And woe to him by whom this offense cometh, for it had been better for him that he had been drowned in the depths of the sea. But blessed are they who have kept the covenant and have observed the commandment, for they shall obtain mercy. (*Doctrine and Covenants* 54:4–6)

We might well ask ourselves, "what kind of person do I have to be to keep my covenants?" Here are four traits that must characterize our innermost selves to keep us covenant-makers rather than covenant-breakers:

1. A true covenant-maker stands responsibly alone with the Lord. Of course, this does not mean that we are supposed to be hermits. It does mean that an individual's covenants have nothing to do with other people: a covenant is made with the Lord. The promise we make in every covenant is very simple: we will not leave the covenant no matter what it should cost us, even if our lives may be taken. There are saints in every dispensation who actually have lost everything, even their lives, in order to stay in the covenant. No less is expected of us.

2. A true covenant-maker does not make excuses. Every covenant-breaker in history believes he or she is justified in leaving covenants. There are several excuses used by scapegoating covenant-breakers throughout time, including "other people in the Church have insulted me," or "this is just too hard to do," or "I just didn't know what I was doing when I made the covenant," etc. Scapegoating and excuse-making are the paranoia of Satanism, and may be clearly recognized as the thorn of guilty conscience piercing the hearts of those not living by the Spirit. The Lord says, "those who have this law revealed unto them must obey the same. For behold, I reveal unto you a new and everlasting covenant; and if ye abide not that covenant, then ye are damned; for no one can reject this covenant and be permitted to enter into my glory" (*Doctrine and Covenants* 132:3–4). "Abiding not that covenant" means leaving a covenant and then trying to justify it. "Abiding that covenant" means joyfully staying in a covenant no matter what it might cost and being concerned with one's own righteousness rather than with that of others.

3. A true covenant-maker lives very close to the Spirit. President David O. McKay identifies living close to the Spirit as the essence of true religion, and there are three manifestations of this aspect of a true covenant-maker (*Secrets of a Happy Life*, 87–90). First of all, there is the spiritual attitude of the individual toward the divine; secondly, worship; and third, service to one's fellow man. A person may conform to the outward forms of relgiosity, ye. not be close to the Spirit. It is living close to

the Holy Spirit that keeps us from the wrong thinking that leads to disastrous consequences, as illustated by the following story told by President McKay:

> In the paper the other morning was an account of a tragedy of a sixty-five-year-old mother who ended her life after a struggle of years to keep her boy from the clutches of the law. She did save him for many years by giving him everything which he demanded. She even scrubbed floors of offices to gratify his selfishness and indulgence. He passed many years without coming in contact with the law, but the crime of wrong thinking was his years ago when he thought that his mother should sacrifice herself for him. (*Secrets of a Happy Life*, 88)

4. A true covenant-maker keeps things in perspective, being careful to meet the muster of covenants, right away and every day, without putting off what is right on principle for the sake of what is convenient in practice. Let me tell you the story of someone I knew in the mission field. He loved missionary work. He worked very hard at it. He was in a mission field where there were almost no baptisms ever. He tracted every day, contacted on the street every day, worked before dawn with the night-watchmen, after dark with the street workers, and during rain, storm, and cold with anyone around. He never baptized anybody. Returning home to school, he was called to work with the Stake mission. He worked there for two years, worked so hard that everything else took second place, worked so hard he had health problems. He never taught anyone who was baptized. Three years after his Stake mission he got married. He was ordained a Seventy (in the old days when there were Seventy in each Stake) and served four years in the Stake Seventy quorum, averaging three nights a week with the full-time missionaries during those years. He even tracted in places where the full-time missionaries did not dare to go. He never taught anyone who was baptized. Three days after being released from his Stake duties his neighbor called and asked him to teach her the Gospel. Six days later that neighbor was baptized. Now, here is the moral of this story. Just because we don't see the results of our commitment doesn't give us an excuse to quit working. Anyone will work hard keeping covenants if he gets immediate rewards and blessings. Even Satan does that. Keeping a covenant is doing what we're supposed to do, when we're supposed to do it, for as long is it takes to do it, whether it is painful to do it or not, without regard to whether or not we are getting a reward.

IV

Remember when Christ was baptized. Just what did he need to make this covenant for? Being holy, He did not need a remission of sins as you and I do. Being perfect, he did not need acceptance into His own Kingdom. Being a God, He did not need to receive the Holy Ghost, he himself being one of the Godhead. The Savior was baptized to exemplify for us that we absolutely need to make covenants and we absolutely need to keep them. Even the Savior "...humbleth himself before the Father, and witnesseth unto the Father that he would be obedient unto him in keeping his commandments" (II Nephi 31:7). To fulfill all righteousness means to do the will of God, whose will it is that we make and keep holy covenants. Elder Boyd K. Packer has said:

> Keeping our covenants will take courage on the part of each of us. It seems that, each generation or so, there comes a period of time when the faithful of the Church are under great criticism, even under attack. This has always been true of those who are under covenant with the Lord. We must expect, as part of our way of life, to stand condemned on occasion by those outside the Church who oppose the standards the Lord has directed us to keep. (*The Holy Temple*, 166)

Keeping our covenants is the very measure of our right to stand with God, the bottom-line of our righteousness. Keeping our covenants is our privilege, our joy. Let us not be corrupted by those around us who refuse to keep the covenants, nor by the weak parts of us that give up when the going gets tough. If we enter God's kingdom having passed through ranks of angels, and if we have a tag pinned to our white clothing, we should hope that tag will have written on it the one true title that will cause our righteous judges to smile with joy: *A Keeper of the Covenants.*

Idea Six: FORGIVENESS

Timorous Tenderness Is Not Enough

It has been wisely pointed out that "as long as man lives in his mortal state, we will be confronted with imperfection, with our main chore to overcome that imperfection" (Elder Robert L. Simpson, *Ensign*, November 1977, 46). Some would argue that a person's imperfections represent "just the way they are," and weak, corrosive men and women "just cannot help it." Of course, this is nonsense: "It can be done. Man can conquer self. Man can overcome. Man can forgive all who have trespassed against him and go on to receive peace in this life and eternal life in the world to come" (*The Miracle of Forgiveness*, 300). That is, not only is it possible, even necessary, for weak and sinful women and men to repent, by changing their behavior and attitudes, confessing before all those affected, and making full emotional and financial restitution, but it is also possible, even necessary, for all affected by the sinner's attitudes and behavior to forgive and go forward without feelings of revenge or hatred.

Christ is the ultimate example of a forgiving heart and mind, and the command to follow him applies in the matter of forgiveness as well as in all other matters facing our daily struggle to overcome the "natural man" in the development of God-like character. Significantly, Heavenly Father has made our forgiving of others a precondition of his forgiving us (*Doctrine and Covenants* 58:42 and III Nephi 13:14–15), so that any hope we have of having our mistake-ridden character cleansed depends not only upon our own repentance, but upon our willingness to forgive others. After all is said and done, the categorical imperative we call the "golden rule" undergirds everything: "do unto others as you would have them do unto you."

President Gordon B. Hinckley emphasizes a great truth when he says:

> We are all prone to brood on the evil done us. That brooding becomes as a gnawing and destructive canker. Is there a virtue more in need of application in our time than the virtue of forgiving and forgetting? There are those who would look upon this as a sign of weakness. Is it? I submit that it takes neither strength nor intelligence to brood in anger over wrongs suffered, to go through life with a spirit of vindictiveness, to dissipate one's abilities planning retribution. There is no peace in the nursing of a grudge. There is no happiness in living for the day when you can "get even." (*Ensign*, November 1980, 62)

For peace and righteousness to reign we must be willing to forgive, because taking offense is a way of giving offense, especially to God.

Jesus, in teaching the first disciples about this principle, clearly explained the connection between sinfulness and forgiveness: "It is impossible but that offenses will come: but woe unto him, through whom they come! It were better for him that a millstone were hanged about his neck, and he cast into the sea, than that he should offend…" (Luke 17:1–2). There is supreme condemnation awaiting those who sin, or who, through their sins, make it difficult for others to live in righteousness. That is the reason we are commanded not to tolerate sin, either in ourselves or others: "Take heed to yourselves: if thy brother trespass against thee, rebuke him…" (Luke 17:3). And we are commanded not to tolerate in ourselves the sin of holding grudges: "And if (thy brother) repent, forgive him. And if he trespass against thee seven times in a day, and seven times in a day turn again to thee saying, I repent; thou shalt forgive him" (Luke 17:3–4). We are under divine decree, first of all, to be intolerant of sin; secondly, to not hold grudges or seek revenge against those who have sinned, trespassed against us, or violated what we stand for; and thirdly, to speak forgiveness to anyone who asks for it, without regard to how many times we may be required to do so. There will be no forgiveness without repentance, and among those begging for forgiveness God will absolve whom he will: but of us it is required to forgive everyone who seeks it (*Doctrine and Covenants* 64:10).

I

Thus, it is clear that forgiveness is one of the great Gospel virtues, and this virtue is a specific ethos of mind and heart revealed in the scriptures and words of the Lord's priesthood leaders. *But in these revelations is no hint that forgiveness is the reflexive indulgence taught and exemplified by the talk-show culture in which we live.* In a society as enamored of "touchy-feely" attitudes about truth, and an "it doesn't really matter" relativism about ethics, there is great pressure on us to provide an unthinking blanket absolution for anything anyone does, no matter how much agony they have inflicted upon others by their behavior, and then mislabel it "forgiveness." The fact is that reflexive exoneration is direct complicity in the sin committed, not the rejection of the sin and healing of the sinner at the core of authentic forgiveness.

Any attitude or behavior on the part of others that allows a person to avoid full responsibility for the pain they have caused by their transgressions is in and of itself another sin added to the original evil. The righteous person is one who knows how to appropriately interact with a sinner when repentance (that is, recognition, remorse, behavioral change, and full restitution) is absent or incomplete. To interact in such a way as to give the impression that what the sinner has done is somehow acceptable is not only not forgiveness, but evil indulgence. No spiritually mature person will tolerate evil in this way: it is cowardice that leads to the blanket absolution of fake forgiveness, cowardice reflected in not standing up to sin and the sinner, not making it absolutely clear that the sin will not be tolerated. Significantly, real compassion for the sinner will always be lost, absorbed in the fear of "offending," "not being accepting," or some other false and tendentious form of selfishness.

Sin and its effects do not exist in a vacuum: they are person and time specific. The evil of sinful behavior has an absolute effect on absolutely particular individuals in absolutely unique circumstances and moments. The offender must offer particularized repentance to particular people for particular harm done. The offended must be prepared to offer specific forgiveness to particular people for particular harm done under particular circumstances. For the person offering forgiveness to generalize the process is to strip it of all meaning. Even worse, generalizing "forgiveness" is complicity in the specific sinner's continuing irresponsibility and specifically harmful behavior. It is often more useful to offer clear forgiveness after specific difficulties have been resolved: otherwise, problematic behavior may never be changed and a cycle of toxic transgression continues to harm and even destroy others. It is true that we must never seek revenge or hold a grudge against anyone because they sin, but it is also true that linking open, public, and specific forgiveness to repentance is deeply compassionate. If a sinner who really desires to repair damage caused by his or her sin realizes that the sinfulness will not be tolerated; if she is aware that, while compassionate, the harmed person is not going to help her sin by being indulgent; then the sinner may get the connection between repentance, forgiveness, and charity. And it is important to remember another specificity, to remind ourselves that forgiveness can only be given by the one sinned against. No person has the moral right to forgive sin done to others.

It is also important to consider the *arrogance* of blanket exoneration. Some may be in the habit of offering "forgiveness" precisely because they are excessively sensitive to what others do to "harm" them, when there is no real harm done. Often it may be more mature to realize that we should offer compassion and understanding rather than so-called "forgiveness." When we are urged to "forgive" we might be wise enough to realize that "forgiveness" is not always possible or even appropriate, that a "sin" against us may be merely a shadow of our own immature hypersensitivity.

Related to the moral flaw of hypersensitivity is the idea that the best reason to forgive someone is that it is emotionally healthy in some way, that forgiving brings "closure," to use a buzz word of our self-indulgent culture. Obviously this is simple egocentrism disguised as religiosity: what is being said is "I forgive you because I deserve to feel better."

The "feel-good" doctrine of blanket exoneration has frightening consequences for the moral development of individuals, because blanket exoneration is based upon the immoral idea that no matter how much we hurt others, everyone will forgive us, so it is okay to continue to sin. If we are automatically forgiven no matter what we do, why change? Here we find the root cause of pathological behavior. No psychopath has difficulty understanding that when we exonerate everybody for the sins they commit, we make deity irrelevant: the "forgiver" has substituted himself for God.

II

Aside from the psychopathology of feel-good "forgiveness," there is the sheer nonsense of blanket exoneration. We can look at it this way. "3 + 8 = 11" is not a true statement. "In a base-ten system 3 + 8 = 11" is a true statement. The first is not true because it assumes one or more contextual parts that may or may not be present. The second is true because it makes clear the issue *and* the context. But the first statement is not true in another way: it assumes "possibility" as "actuality" (the assumption is that the speaker of the phrase "must be" talking about a base-ten system). The second is true because it is a contextual absolute (it "recognizes" that there is a difference between "possibly" and "absolutely"). "3 + 8 = 11" is *possibly* true (if we can assume a base-ten system), but there is no evidence that it is *absolutely* true until all the facts of the statement are present. The same thing is true of statements such as "apples are red."

Note that in the same way "we must forgive everyone" is a very problematic idea, because it implies that the sinner has repented and asked for forgiveness, an assumption tantamount to acceptance of unrepentant sin. "We must be prepared to forgive everyone while holding no grudges," on the other hand, makes clear the issue and the context.

Perhaps the basic issue is that everything has consequences, as we know from a consideration of the law of the harvest. So, for example, if a person has not sinned, then he does not need forgiveness. But if a person *has* sinned and *has repented* openly (has confessed and made restitution), then he will have, by definition, asked for forgiveness and we will grant it without thoughts of revenge or moral superiority. However, if a person *has* sinned and *has not repented* (openly confessed and made restitution), then we must hold no grudge against him while he is going through the repentance process, and we must lovingly speak forgiveness to him when he asks for it. There is a categorical difference between "we must be forgiving" or "we must be prepared to forgive" on the one hand, and "we must blindly exonerate" on the other.

III

In speaking of faith and hope, President Howard W. Hunter said:

> (It) is not a Pollyanna-like approach to significant personal and public problems. I don't believe we can wake up in the morning and simply by drawing a big "happy face" on the chalkboard believe that is going to take care of the world's difficulties. But if our faith and hope are anchored in Christ, in his teachings, commandments, and promises, then we are able to count on something truly remarkable, genuinely miraculous, which can part the Red Sea and lead modern Israel... (*That We Might Have Joy*, 95)

Obviously, there is great wisdom here, and the application of President Hunter's principle seems clear. It will not help anyone to deal with forgiveness in a Pollyanna-like manner, where we think we can simply draw a happy face on the difficulties sinners cause in the world and believe that somehow that face will smile sin away. Our forgiveness must be anchored in Christ's example and teachings, his commandments and promises, before we can expect the power of forgiveness to make a difference in this world.

Otherwise nice and well-meaning Christians substitute blanket indulgence and generalized acceptance for true forgiveness for a number of reasons, several of which seem to be rampant.

1. Blanket exoneration keeps a person from confronting sin for what it is and evil-doers for who they are. It engenders phrases such as

"hate the sin, love the sinner," an undeniable truth that often seems used, unfortunately, in such a way as to imply that what people do is separate from who they are. It is right to have charity for every individual, but it is wrong to invoke "charity" as a way to ignore sin and its effects. Love is not an acceptance of everything.

2. Blanket exoneration insulates a person from confronting and overcoming the emotional pain caused by specific sinners committing specific misdeeds that impact specific people in specific ways. Non-confrontational ways of dealing with emotional trauma are counterproductive because they substitute the need to assuage the hurt feelings of the potential forgiver for the reality of what has actually happened outside the self.

3. Blanket exoneration is often a cover-up for a sinned-against person's refusal to acknowledge her own transgressions. In this case, blanket exoneration is an attitude that says, "I am a sinner and do not want anybody to start probing my weaknesses, so if I just treat others' sins as nothing, then mine will become nothing."

4. Blanket exoneration empowers sinners to keep on sinning while receiving no compassion from others.

5. Blanket exoneration is a form of instant gratification for something that actually takes time and immense patience. The "instant gratification" crowd thinks something like this: "Let's just forgive everybody now so that we don't have to think about it any more or do anything about anything anymore."

6. Blanket exonerators act as though their "accepting" attitude will absolve them of any responsibility to deal with particular sinners in particular ways.

Of course, all these types of fake forgiveness are related, and all come from simple-mindedness about evil as well as from spiritual torpor. But real forgiveness can be given, and it can have great power, if the potential forgiver is willing to overcome self-centeredness and live by the principles of truth rather than by worries about what others may say or do. As an example of this I quote a letter sent by a seventeen-year-old daughter to her mother, after the mother had filed for divorce from her father, and submitted as part of an assignment in a university course on ethical behavior.

> Dear Mom:
>
> I want you to know that I love you and I always will. What I have to say in this letter is not because I hate you or want to harm you. In fact, I am writing this letter because I want what is best for you.
>
> Because I love you, I want you to know that you will have to admit what you have done to our family and make amends for it, before we can ever have a good relationship again. The great and horrible sins you have committed do not allow me to associate with you in any normal way. You filed for divorce, and so broke your temple covenants and destroyed our family. Then, you have spent years trying to scapegoat people and circumstances for your decision. You continually make excuses to try to justify what you did, and that only compounds the betrayal of your covenants that ripped our family apart.
>
> I hope you are a big enough person to make a public confession that your filing for divorce has permanently ruined what used to be our family, and that your continual efforts over the years to justify your decision are wrong and evil. As I say, I love you. But I love the Lord too, and cannot have loyalty to someone who has destroyed our family by leaving the covenant. Please show responsibility and maturity so that I can again have a relationship with you.
>
> Love, Elizabeth

Instead of tiptoeing around the issue, this mature and brave young woman confronted her mother about her sin. Instead of trying to avoid the issue at hand by saying to herself such things as "Well, I cannot judge what happened, so I'll be accepting of everybody involved," she faced reality on its own terms. Instead of playing the part of Pollyanna, she played the part of righteous daughter of God. Instead of being intimidated about what her mother might say, or how she might react, she behaved in a principled way. And the miracle is that eventually her mother repented! This daughter's bravery linked forgiveness and compassion with righteous judgment and personal integrity, and helped save a soul from the permanence of damnation.

III

We must remember that Satan "wins," not just by helping people commit overt evil, but by helping people countenance sin as without consequence. *He does not have to get us to sin so much as to be accepting of others' particular sins or of sinning in general.* Getting us to think of forgiveness as blanket indulgence and non-confrontational exoneration is one of the ways in which he maintains his rule of horror on this earth.

It is absolutely true that we must forgive those who ask to be forgiven. It is also absolutely true that we must be prepared to speak forgiveness to anyone who may at some future time ask for forgiveness. It is also absolutely true that if someone has sinned against us and has never asked for forgiveness we will never, under any circumstances, hold a grudge against him or have anything but compassion in our minds and hearts. But it is difficult to attach any descriptor other than "wicked" to the idea that we must forgive everybody as a prior act, as though we were God, as though sin is without consequence, and as though forgiveness is some kind of generalized, and thus meaningless, sentiment. It is absolutely true that when we indulge in such a sentiment, sin wins and Satan is gleeful at yet another one of our self-indulgences. Forgiveness is always linked to love, and *the only way to show love is to reject its counterfeits*: mere acceptance, enabling, and timidity.

Idea Seven: READING THE SCRIPTURES

With An Eye Single to Searching

The subject of "How to Read the Scriptures" is more than a matter of which color the covers should be, how much we should spend to purchase them, and what ingenious methods we will strain to invent for a marking system—it is a matter of the deepest penetration of the Spirit into the mind and heart of an individual. One day in a Book of Mormon course two students were in a lively discussion over what sort of paper was best to print scriptures on, and whether or not it was really economical to purchase the expensive kind done on India paper or if the cheaper kind would do. Out of the blue, one of the young men across the room simply said: "Yes, but the thing is, do we actually spend enough time reading the scriptures for all this to make any difference anyway?" A telling question, it seems. Four parts to the problem of reading the scriptures suggest themselves.

I

There is, first of all, the question, "What is Scripture?" And there is, like most questions, a fairly straightforward answer. It is found in the 68th section of the *Doctrine and Covenants*, verse 4. "And whatsoever they shall speak when moved upon by the Holy Ghost shall be scripture, shall be the will of the Lord, shall be the mind of the Lord, shall be the word of the Lord, shall be the voice of the Lord, and the power of God unto salvation." Note very carefully what this verse actually says. It does not matter what is said: as long as it is said under the influence of the Holy Ghost then it is scripture. Note what scripture is called: the will, mind, word, and voice of *the Lord*, not the person uttering it. And what is it for? Scripture contains the power of God unto salvation; that is, it is absolutely necessary for us to have in order to be saved.

Of course, there is a difference between scripture and The Scriptures. The difference is essentially this: out of all the statements made by the Lord through mortal men via the inspiration of the Holy Ghost, some are designated to be formalized in such a way as to be passed on as a people for all people. This formalization creates The Scriptures, and is the reason why they are the authorized statements by which we measure the present against the past. Let us not forget that there are many scriptural utterings not in The Scriptures.

These have power and are authoritative just as The Scriptures' scripture is. They should be studied too. But only when scripture is formalized into the canon of The Scriptures is it for passing on to all mankind for the Lord's particular purposes. Remember the many instances in The Scriptures when the Lord commands the brethren to keep historical, philosophical, and literary records? For example Moses 6:5–6 and 45–46; Abraham 1:28–31; *Doctrine and Covenants* 21:1; 2 Nephi 29:7–14. We learn the same truth from them all, namely that one of the reasons we keep records of our inspirational doings and sayings because *some of them* will be *canonized* and *passed on* to future generations.

II

Second of all, there is the question, "What has the Lord told us about reading scripture and The Scriptures?" Elder James E. Talmage was inspired to say:

> In the short span of mortal existence it is impossible for man to explore with thoroughness any considerable part of the vast realm of knowledge. It becomes, therefore, the part of wisdom to direct our efforts to the investigation of the field that promises results of greatest worth. All truth is of value, above price indeed in its place; yet, with respect to their possible application some truths are of incomparably greater worth than others. A knowledge of the principles of trade is essential to the success of the merchant; and acquaintance with the laws of navigation is demanded of the mariner; familiarity with the relation of soil and crops is indispensable to the farmer; and understanding of the principles of mathematics is necessary to the engineer and the astronomer; so too is a personal knowledge of God essential to the salvation of every human soul that has attained to powers of judgment and discretion. The value of theological (scriptural) knowledge, therefore, ought not to be underrated; it is doubtful if its importance can be over-estimated. (*Articles of Faith* 4)

President Gordon B. Hinckley speaks powerfully about the need for reading, knowledge, and clear-thinking in this way:

> Our world needs straightening up. It needs leadership. It needs enlightenment. It needs those who are able to analyze problems and suggest solutions, those who can draw upon the past to make intelligent decisions for the future, those who understand the ramifications of certain kinds of actions, those who appreciate fully the interplay between virtue and morality and integrity and the fabric of society. (*Standing for Something* 64)

The prophets have instructed us to gain as much knowledge as possible, and to do so for a number of reasons, but to remember that scriptural knowledge is a cornerstone. This reminds us of Brigham Young's editorial in the 7 February 1852 issue of the *Deseret News*:

> "Some have supposed that it would make but little difference with them whether they learned much or little, whether they attained to all the intelligence within their reach or not while they tarry in this world, believing that if they paid their tithing, went to meetings, said their prayers, and performed those duties which were especially commanded, that it would be well with them and that as soon as they lay off this mortal body all would be well with them. But this is a mistaken idea and will cause every soul to mourn who embraces and practices upon it. When they arrive in the world of resurrected bodies, they will realize, to their sorrow that God required of them in this world not only obedience to His revealed will, but searching after His purposes and plans.

Elder Orson Pratt defined an orthodox Latter-day Saint in this way:

> We are commanded over and over again to treasure up (all) wisdom in our hearts, continually, to treasure up the words of eternal life continually, and make ourselves acquainted with not only the ancient revelations, but with the modern; to make ourselves acquainted not only with things pertaining to time, but with things pertaining to eternity. (The faithful and diligent Latter-day Saint) is not the ill-instructed scribe, not the person who does not study, not the person who suffers his time to run to idleness, but is that man that instructs himself in all things within his reach so far as his circumstances and abilities will allow. (*Masterful Discourses and Writings of Orson Pratt* 28)

You see, one could say that it is difficult to be an orthodox Latter-day Saint if one does not spend a good deal of time studying every day, not just the scriptures, but especially the scriptures. We are reminded of the straight rebuke Jesus gave to those who did not know the scriptures. Reread Matthew 22:29 and Luke 24:25–27, 44–46 for a real eye opener. If it is true that we cannot be saved in ignorance, cannot be exalted without the knowledge and the skills gained by studying everything and especially the scriptures (*Doctrine and Covenants* 131:6 and 2nd Timothy 3:15), then it is thoughtless and irresponsible not to study.

III

Thirdly, there is the question, "What is reading?" We could arrive at a standard definition of literacy and intelligence as "to gain a large share of information about and understanding of the world and the eternities from the written word." There seems to be a feeling nowadays that reading is not as necessary as it once was. Radio, TV, and other visual media have taken over many of the functions once served by print. Admittedly, these media, especially TV, serve some of these functions well; the visual communication of news events, for example, has enormous impact. The ability of radio to give us information while we are engaged in doing other things—for instance, driving a car—is remarkable, and a great saving of time. But it may be seriously questioned whether the advent of modern communications media has enhanced our understanding of the world in which we live, to say nothing of the eternities in which we hope to live.

In other words, it may be argued (even though many of these arguments are totally unconvincing) that we know more about the world than we used to. If knowledge is a prerequisite to understanding, then that is all to the good. But knowledge is not so much a prerequisite to understanding as is commonly supposed. We do not have to know everything about something to understand it. In fact, being inundated with factual knowledge often hinders understanding. The best example of this is just the situation we are in with the modern media. Radio, TV, etc. (especially TV), is so designed as to make thinking seem unnecessary. This is how it is done, in case any of us are actually fooled by the charade.

In order to fit news, for example, into the structure of TV programming, everything has to be packaged. This packaging of intellectual positions and views is one of the most active enterprises of some of the most clever minds of our day. The viewer of television, the listener to radio, even the reader of magazines, is presented with a whole complex of elements—all the way from ingenious rhetoric to carefully selected data and statistics—to make it easy for him to make up his mind with a minimum of difficulty and effort. The packaging is done so effectively that the viewer, the listener, etc. does not make up his own mind at all. Instead, he inserts a packaged opinion into his mind, somewhat like inserting a compact disk into a CD player. He then pushes a button and "plays back" the opinion whenever it seems appropriate to do so. He has performed without having had to think.

Now, it could create difficulties if this is the mentality that informs some of the approach to the scriptures found among members of the Church. Instead of actually reading the scriptures in all their complexity, historical detail, literary multidimensionality, and philosophical density, we sometimes take secondary literary and commentative bestsellers which can give us packaged interpretations to plug into our so-called "thinking" and thus have an acceptable series of lines to say without ever having had to think about the scriptures at all. I am reminded of the missionary who, in a meeting, wondered why his mission president did not let the missionaries have any books to read except the scriptures. "Surely," the missionary said, "there are good things in the books published by Church-friendly outlets. Why do we have to stick to the scriptures?" The reply: "Elder, if you really knew the scriptures like you should, you could write all those books yourself." You see, we do not need to have others package in any sense the things we can learn better by just studying the scriptures.

Reading is an activity. Therefore, reading must be active and not passive. Many people think that, as compared with writing and speaking, reading and listening are passive. In other words, the writer and speaker must put forth some effort, but no effort is needed to read or listen. Reading and listening are thought of as passively receiving information from someone who is actively giving it. This is false. The reader is like the catcher in a game of baseball, where catching is just as much an active mode as throwing. The art of catching, like reading, is the skill of catching every kind of pitch—fast balls, curves, sliders, those that drop into the dirt, changeups, knuckleballs. To be a good reader takes an intellectual coordination and training, a "mental athleticness," as it were, analogous to being a first-rate athlete in the physical realm. The written word, ready to be received in its complexity by a skilled mental "athlete," formalizes communication and is a highly-skilled, formalized, essential antidote to casualness. You can immediately see what I mean if you can visualize a person sitting down to read in a quiet environment, concentrating with prayer on every word of the scriptures, pencil and paper in hand to thoughtfully go over details and make comments, and so forth—with the other person who glibly puts the *Book of Mormon* CD in the CD player so that it can play in the background while he cheerfully goes about washing the car or watching a TV soap-opera.

IV

In the fourth place, there is the question, "Just exactly how does one read the scriptures?" Let me make three suggestions.

First of all, we must read with common sense. We have all heard scriptural passages read with foolishly unrealistic twistings. The key idea here is to read just what the scriptures say, with the obvious explanation of what they mean giving us answers, and not to trick out some meaning that fits our preconceived notions. For example, it is amusing how adroitly some Bible believers can be in explaining away the New Testament statement on baptism for the dead. The fact is that the scriptures say that Christianity practices baptism for the dead. There is no argument about this, that is just what the scriptures say. All you have to do is read it. And the fact that what the scripture says does not fit some people's preconceived idea about what the scriptures are supposed to say does not change the fact that the scriptures say what they say.

Second, we must read with *hunger*. I remember my son learning to catch a ball. He has become very good at it because he wanted to do it so badly that he spent time every day doing it. He got hit in the face with it, fell down going after it, skinned his arms and legs tripping after it, got a sore arm doing it. But he wanted to learn to do it, so he did. We must hunger after reading the scriptures enough to sweat, pray, fast, reread, pray, reread, work, reread.

Third, we might follow *Joseph Smith's rule of reading*:

> I have a key by which I understand the scriptures. I inquire, what was the question which drew out the answer, or....(for example) caused Jesus to utter the parable....To ascertain its meaning, we must dig up the root and ascertain what it was that drew the saying out. (*Teachings of the Prophet Joseph Smith* 276–77)

In other words, we must read in the context of the text's origin. There is some obvious reason why any scriptural passage is there in the first place. We can ask ourselves, "what is this reason?" That is, what is the obvious thing behind why this is in here? What is the root of this? Also, we must read the mode that is actually there. If we do not read with reference to the nature of the writing in the passage at hand, we shall never grasp what significance the passage has. There are three main modes in the scriptures: literary, historical, and philosophical. We must read literary passages as literature, historical passages as history, philosophical passages as theological writing. What happens when we do not do this can be imagined by thinking of a person reading a newspaper as though it were a Shakespearean sonnet, of reading Aristotle as though it were ancient history, or reading a textbook on American history as though it were canonized scripture. You can see that this kind of reading would not only lead to misunderstanding, but would be a perversion of the very nature of the doctrine found in various passages.

We must insist that we read the scriptures, for we must know what is in the present canon to be ready for the "great and important things pertaining to the kingdom" which are yet to be revealed. The scriptures are a never ending activity, just like reading itself never ends.

Idea Eight: FATHERHOOD

Facts and Fictions

Sometimes we get caught up in the details of the moment and obscure (or entirely forget) the details of the eternities. Our lives can become exercises in "quiet desperation," in loss of our eternal identity. Unhappiness, depression, destructive habits of thinking and feeling, and hopelessness can result. Of all matters revealed to us by Heavenly Father that get obscured by our historical moment's loss of perspective, fatherhood seems to be one of the most out of focus. Pondering this matter helps us see if there are ideas and feelings needing a close examination.

I

The first relationship on earth was established by our Heavenly

Father when he gave Eve to Adam in marriage (Moses 4:21–24). The second relationship was established when Adam and Eve were commanded to have children (to "multiply and replenish the earth"). Since then, each of us has been commanded to marry and have children so that through our own experience we can learn to be heavenly spouses and parents. Brigham Young explained that our spouses and children are not yet ours: Heavenly Father has committed them to us for this moment in mortality in order to see how we will treat them (*Gospel Principles*, Chapter Two). Only if we are personally faithful to every covenant we make will our spouses be given to us forever and our children be connected to our patriarchal line. What we do on earth absolutely determines whether or not we shall have our spouses in the eternities and whether or not our children shall be in our eternal family.

Everything is a matter of righteousness. Fatherhood, therefore, is not a function of biology, but a function of Priesthood, where a man's righteousness is measured. One is not a father simply because one biologically procreates a child—one is a father because one spiritually takes responsibility for a child (the same is true of motherhood). *No man or woman can have a child connected to his Priesthood line unless he/she lives up to every covenant he has made.*

In other words, family relationships are, in the end, covenant-determined, not biologically determined, a fact the world has completely obscured. Biological relationships provide testing opportunites during mortality, but are not guaranteed for the eternities. It is clear that a person's father or mother is he or she to whom a child is assigned in a patriarchal lineage, based upon righteousness, and this eternal connection may or may not have some relationship to mortal biology. If a father or a mother breaks his or her covenants through overt sin or abandonment, he or she has failed the test, and biological connections are not determinate. In other words, a biological forbear is not a father or mother unless he/she keeps the covenant. A child's father or mother is the man or woman who has been assigned in the covenant to be the patriarch and matriarch of the family through his or her righeousness. In fact, to use the terms "father" and "mother" in reference to anyone who has abandoned the covenant is inappropriate for those who have an understanding of the eternities. It is useful to remember that a biological parent is not yet an eternal one, and it is spiritually immature to use language in such a way as to imply that they are.

A biological forebear can lose his or her family relationships by breaking or abandoning the covenant, and it is important to remember that such a person can repent and again be eligible for all priesthood blessings, including eternal increase. But if, in the meantime, the biological parent who remained faithful to the covenant, who did not commit excommunicatable sin or abandon the covenant through divorce or desertion, is sealed to another, who remains faithful, the covenant-breaker might expect his/her eternal parenthood to be problematic at best, cancelled at worst.

We need to remember that righteousness is a matter of choice. We came to this earth by our own choice. We knew in leaving our heavenly home, where we were surrounded by light, glory, knowledge, and perfect love, that there would be risk. We understood that mortality, this second estate, was absolutely crucial to our further progress in the eternities. By leaving the premortal existence, we voluntarily entered another time of proving, a proving centered specifically on being a spouse and a parent. God said:

> And we will prove them herewith, to see if they will do all things whatsoever the Lord their God shall command them. And they who keep their first estate shall be added upon; and they who keep not their first estate shall not have glory in the same kingdom with those who keep their first estate; and they who keep their second estate shall have glory added upon their heads forever and ever (Abraham 3:25–26).

To repeat, the specific way in which Heavenly Father proves a man is to give him opportunity to have an earthly family patterned exactly after Heavenly Father's eternal family. Whether a man will be privileged to be a husband and father in eternity depends upon how he conducts himself towards his earthly family specifically according to the covenants he has made.

"Father" means patriarch. A patriarch is the leader of a Priesthood order established in the days of Adam and Eve (*Doctrine and Covenants* 107:41). This order of the Priesthood is called, therefore, the "Patriarchal Order" and is the actual structure of the universe. That is, this Priesthood order is patterned according to the way the universe is organized. Each of us will be assigned to a father in this order in the eternities entirely according to righteousness in the covenant.

II

The Oath and Covenant of the Priesthood (*Doctrine and Covenants* 84) suggests that before being a good father a man must be a good husband (the same is exactly true for wives and mothers). Reversing the priorities of the two roles is a formula for disaster. The Oath and Covenant of the Priesthood also tells us how to be a good spouse and then a good parent. Listen carefully to the "whats" and "hows" of this covenant:

> For whoso is faithful unto the obtaining of these two priesthoods of which I have spoken [the Aaronic and the Melchizedek], and the magnifying their calling [as husbands and fathers], are sanctified by the Spirit unto the renewing of their bodies. (*Doctrine and Covenants* 84:33)

The health and strength can be mortal as well as eternal, all depending upon how we keep our promises.

> And also all they who receive this priesthood receive me, saith the Lord; for he that receiveth my servants [husbands and fathers received by wives and children] receiveth me; and he that receiveth me receiveth my Father; and he that receiveth my Father receiveth my Father's kingdom; therefore all that my Father hath shall be given unto him. And this is according to the oath and covenant which belongeth to the priesthood. (*Doctrine and Covenants* 84:35–39)

Nobody comes into the Lord's kingdom without receiving a husband and father righteously functioning in the Oath and Covenant of the Priesthood. To receive means to follow, to cherish, to seek counsel, to sustain, to be loyal. There is no way for wives and children to come into the celestial kingdom without being fully connected to the Priesthood in this way: the responsibility for absolute fidelity is sacrosanct. That is the reason for the Lord's condemnation of unrighteous Priesthood bearers, those who have broken their covenants in any way:

> Therefore, all those who receive the priesthood, receive this oath and covenant of my Father, which he cannot break, neither can it be moved. But whoso, breaketh this covenant after he hath received it,

> and altogether turneth therefrom [for example, by sexual sin or sin against the Holy Ghost], shall not have forgiveness of sins in this world nor in the world to come. (*Doctrine and Covenants* 84:40–41)

The responsibility to fidelity to the Priesthood covenants is solely that of a husband and father: if he goes astray it absolutely cannot be anyone else's fault.

Let us rivet a principle in our hearts and minds once and for all. Being a celestial husband and father depends upon the Priesthood. The Priesthood is the power and authority of God used among men to bring about God's purposes. His chief purpose is to prepare us to be eternal spouses: His secondary purpose is to prepare us to be eternal parents. The power and authority of God is given to us chiefly to be husbands and fathers. A husband and father, therefore, must know God's purposes for family members and then do what can be done to bring them about—this is precisely a husband and father's calling. This is the reason a righteous husband and father receives revelation for the family about what to do, how to do it, to sense when something is wrong (and when something is right), and so on. This requires selflessness, humility, and courage. It requires a husband/father to stand for the right no matter what it costs. A husband/father serves his wife and children, and they are absolutely loyal to his righteousness and leadership.

Let us not forget that the Priesthood can be lost: that is, the power and authority to act in the name of God for the welfare of family members can be taken away. Nothing could be worse than losing the power of God to bring about God's purposes especially for the family. The Lord is clear on how a man can lose the Priesthood: "No power or influence can or ought to be maintained by virtue of the priesthood, only by persuasion, by long suffering, by gentleness and meekness, and by love unfeigned; by kindness, and pure knowledge, which shall greatly enlarge the soul without hypocrisy, and without guile" (*Doctrine and Covenants* 121:41–42). No husband/father can help bring to pass God's purposes for family members without these qualities of mind and heart: no husband/father can fail to bring to bear God's power in the lives of family members with these qualities.

Perhaps we ought to be reminded that wives in a certain sense share in the Priesthood: indeed, that is what the New and Everlasting Covenant(s) are about. Wives and mothers can lose their part in the power of the Priesthood too, and for the same reasons just mentioned. In fact, it might be useful to outline how a person, either male or female, can lose one's eternal relationships (to lose "righteous dominion," as the scriptures call it, or to indulge in "unrighteous dominion").

Dominion and Order are always lost the same way, by the exercise of unrighteous dominion. If we wish to lose the Priesthood, our spousehood, and our parenthood, here is what we can do. We can manipulate family members; any way will do, by active anger or passive-aggressively. We can become sullen and retreat. We can blame our spouse for our unhappiness. We can refuse to follow. We can refuse to lead. We can become preoccupied and forget to seek Priesthood blessings. We can refuse to give Priesthood blessings. We can show our disrespect by being light-minded about sacred things. We can show our disrespect by back-talk. We can share personal and sacred things outside the marriage relationship. We can put pressure on our children to succeed according to the world's standards and goals. In fact, we can do anything that violates what the eighty-fourth and one hundred twenty-first sections of the *Doctrine and Covenants* tell us. It is possible, through serious sin without repentance, to lose our authority to be a husband and father, wife and mother. And when it is lost, it does not matter whether man's laws and biological connections continue to define a person as a husband and wife, mother or father—he or she is not one.

III

King Benjamin gave some powerful advice about what to teach children (Mosiah 4: 9–30). Let us listen to him by way of a comparison with what we are actually teaching our children each day. "Believe in God; believe that he is, and that he created all things, both in heaven and in earth; believe that he has all wisdom, and all power, both in heaven and in earth." And here is one to ponder: "Believe that man doth not comprehend all the things which the Lord can comprehend." And do we teach the following clearly enough? "Believe that ye must repent of your sins and forsake them, and humble yourselves before God; and ask in sincerity of heart that he would forgive you..." Here is something we ought to teach with all power and persuasion: "I would that ye should remember, and always retain in remembrance, the greatness of God, and your own nothingness, and his goodness and long suffering towards you … and humble yourselves even in the depths of humility, calling on the name of the Lord daily, and standing steadfastly in the faith of that which is to come…" Heavenly Father, through King Benjamin, also tells us to teach this: "Ye will not have a mind to injure one another, but to live peaceably…" We are not to "suffer [*suffer* means *tolerate*] [our] children that they go hungry, or naked; neither will ye suffer that they transgress the laws of God, and fight and quarrel one with another…" When we tolerate these things between us as spouses, or between us and our children, or between our children themselves, that is the specific way we "serve the devil, who is the master of sin" and "the enemy to all righteousness." Above all, we are to teach our children "to walk in the ways of truth and soberness, (teaching) them to love one another and serve one another." And we teach these things in "wisdom and order" that our children may have individual strength in the Spirit, may learn to stand on their own independent of their earthly father and mother's dominion, so that they may exercise power in their own dominion when they leave childhood. The purpose of Priesthood leadership, especially in the family, is to teach children to be strong enough in the Spirit to be independent of the dominion of earthly parents.

Might we note, just in passing, that children have very clear responsibilities, too? A clue to the nature of these responsibilities is found in Matthew 7:7–9. Children must take the initiative to reject unrighteousness and seek out righteous Priesthood counsel. They must learn to have principles of right and wrong govern their feelings instead of letting their emotions or peer-group assumptions color the way they think and feel about absolute right and wrong.

IV

There are, in spite of what the world likes to teach, responsibilities to fatherhood that cannot be ignored, shifted, or defined out of existence. The Lord has declared it (see, for example such insights as found in *Teachings of David O. McKay*), and He will not be mocked. The father is the patriarch of the family and has important responsibilities that are his alone. He is the head of his home. He is the leader of his family. He must lead and guide with humility and kindness and firmness and fearlessness rather than with force or cruelty or weakness or hand-wringing. It is his duty to earn the living for his family (*Doctrine and Covenants* 75:28), providing necessary (but not excessive) food, housing, and clothing. He is the chief example of keeping the commandments. He presides at family prayer, prayers at the table, home evening, and when company is in the home. He shares Priesthood blessings with members of his family.

The poet Derek Walcott, in speaking of the power of his long-dead father's example ("A Letter From Brooklyn"), forcefully echoes the truth that a father's influence has a ripple effect forever, "as touch a line, and the whole web will feel."

> The strength of one frail hand in a dim room
> Somewhere in Brooklyn, patient and assured,
> Restores my sacred duty…
> (*Collected Poems 1948–1984*, 41–42)

My experience as son, father, and grandfather underscores poetic and scriptural truths about fatherhood, especially two inevitable verities that ring again and again, and that seem especially important for pondering. First of all, anyone who makes it difficult for a righteous man to be a full-time father is an agent of the Adversary. Secondly, nothing is more wicked than a bad father—nothing is as powerful as a good father.

Idea Nine: HAPPINESS

How to Get the Guiding Light Without Becoming a Character in a Soap Opera

We live in a day in which "being happy" is a virtual obsession. Unfortunately, the Lord's doctrine of happiness finds little understanding and almost no acceptance in human society in general. We live in a "therapeutic culture," where the idea that human beings are sinners in need of salvation has been replaced by the notion that we are simply maladjusted and in need of therapy. The eternal truth is that we are without complete knowledge and behave in a weak, selfish way, thus requiring divine intervention and forgiveness. This verity does not sit well with therapeutic gurus, whose sham counsel would have us believe that the highest human achievement is to "feel good about ourselves," since we cannot really change "the way we are." In short, we live in an outrageously narcissistic time in which the accepted wisdom is that with the right therapy, a bunch of sharply-marketed self-help books, and by creating our own feel-good space we shall come to some kind of inner stress-managed condition, the ultimate human purpose. There are no longer any "bad" people—only "sick" ones. And this is supposed to suffice for happiness.

But six principles and four suggestions proceeding from that which has been revealed about real happiness can be made, giving us something to ponder and, hopefully, to use as we identify some reasons why we search incessantly for happiness only to be disappointed again and again.

I

We begin with an emphasis on the basic principles.

Principle Number One: Satan wants us to be unhappy. Even a little pouting, a little scapegoating, a bit of uneasiness will do for the adversary. Satan's primary tool is to persuade us to govern our behavior by unhappiness and depression rather than cheerfulness, happiness, and joy.

Principle Number Two: Life is not a soap opera. Our feelings cannot be properly read in the superficial way presented in sudsy media productions. Sentimentality, or the overweening display of and influence by emotion, is not acceptable to the Lord. His admonition to search, ponder, and pray does not say "be thoughtfully touchy-feely."

Principle Number Three: Being happy is a commandment. It might serve a useful purpose to read through the standard works from time to time looking for the doctrine of happiness: many of us might be very surprised by what we find.

Principle Number Four: Happiness is a decision, not a feeling. One of the most debilitating attitudes of our time is that good feelings precede right decisions. The Lord teaches that good feelings come after right decisions have been made. If you want to feel happy, you must first decide to be happy.

Principle Number Five: Unhappiness is arrogant. Who are we to think that our lot is so difficult or our problems so profound that we have the right to be unhappy? Nothing could be more satanic than this self-indulgence. There is always someone worse off than we are, and Satan would have us forget that.

Principle Number Six: Unhappiness and depression come because we sin. Remember what the great prophet taught in the tenth chapter of Moroni:

> Wherefore, there must be faith; and if there must be faith there must also be hope; and if there must be hope there must also be charity. And except ye have charity ye can in nowise be saved in the kingdom of God; neither can ye be saved in the kingdom of God if ye have not faith; neither can ye if ye have no hope. And if ye have no hope ye must needs be in despair, and despair cometh because of iniquity. (Moroni 10: 21–22)

You see, no person or circumstance is responsible for our feelings. We are responsible for our feelings. You are responsible for how you feel, happy or unhappy, and if you do not feel happy it may be because in some way you are living in iniquity.

Now, if we are going to return to God's presence, we must do so in joy. If we are unhappy, then, we need a "mighty change" in our hearts. And this is the mighty change of which God speaks:

> And they all cried with one voice, saying: Yea, we believe all the words thou hast spoken unto us; and also, we know of their surety and truth, because of the Spirit of the Lord Omnipotent, which has wrought a mighty change in us, or in our hearts, that we have no more disposition to do evil, but to do good continually. (Mosiah 5:2)

Can we all cry with one voice that we have no more disposition to do evil but to do good continually? Can we return to God's presence because we have experienced this mighty change of heart? If we have to admit "no" to this, we have received the first great clue to why we are unhappy. Recall something spoken by President David O. McKay in the April conference of 1962:

> No man can sincerely resolve to apply in his daily life the teachings of Jesus of Nazareth without sensing a change in his own nature. The phrase "born again" has a deeper significance than many people attach to it. This changed feeling may be indescribable, but it is real.(7)

As a matter of fact, as President Benson has said (Melchizedek Priesthood Manual 4, chapter 4), "this change of heart, this born again into joy, is best described in the keystone of our religion, the Book of Mormon." Is this not, indeed, the purpose of all the scriptures? Sometimes it is astonishing that we can read the scriptures without understanding this simple doctrine: that the purpose of living the gospel, studying the scriptures, praying every day, holding family home evening, and all the rest of it is so that we can be happy, so that we have not only no more disposition to do evil but no more disposition to be unhappy and depressed. Think again of the fourth chapter of Alma which describes a period in Nephite history when the church began to fail in its progress. Alma met this challenge by resigning his seat as chief judge in government and confining himself wholly to the high priesthood responsibility which was his, and so he bore down, as it says in the scriptures, "in pure testimony against the people" (Alma 4:19). Why? Because they were sinful? Yes, but probably also because they were unhappy, because they stood around wringing their hands, because they had that depressed look on their faces that comes from sin. And speaking frankly to the members of the church, Alma declared, "I ask of you, my brethren of the church, have ye spiritually been born of God? Have ye received his image in your countenances? Have ye experienced this mighty change in your hearts?" (Alma 5:14). We must understand that until we receive his image in our countenances we cannot be truly happy. If we ask ourselves how important this mighty change in our hearts actually is, we might also ask ourselves if we have experienced this change. And if we have asked ourselves those two questions and we find ourselves lacking (that is, unhappy), then the question is this: what is preventing us from making this mighty change in your hearts? We can understand the concept of spiritual rebirth, or a rebirth from unhappiness to happiness, by studying carefully the twenty-sixth chapter of Mosiah: the change which we must undergo is described in verses twenty-five and twenty-six. And if we add to that the thirty-sixth chapter of Alma, the eleventh chapter of Third Nephi and the seventy-sixth section of the *Doctrine and Covenants,* we shall understand exactly how we can cause this change to come to our lives.

II

So the doctrine of joy is clear. Let us now look at some practical aspects of unhappiness, as a guide to living in the world and not being of it. It is sad but also interesting that depression has always been considered a disease of life's middle or later years, but the medical community now reports a surprising surge in cases among younger people. In point of fact, nowadays there has been a three-fold increase in depression, that is, serious unhappiness, among people in their middle and later years, and a ten-fold increase in depression, even clinical depression, among younger people. The medical community asks why depression strikes earlier and more often now than it has ever before in our history, and in fact the medical profession does not know the precise cause. Numerous explanations have been offered: anxiety and personality disorders; tremendous social changes in the last twenty years, including the shifting roles of men and women; the acceleration of geographic movement that separates people from the support of their families and friends; and so on. It is well to be cautioned against taking the medical community's attempt to explain depression and unhappiness as the only or final word on the matter. While it is true that clinical depression, which can be very serious, requires the attention of a psychiatrist trained to treat the disorder, the fact is that there are daily and weekly things that we can do to help ourselves be joyful and happy. These things are practical steps to be taken and assume the true transcendental and spiritual understanding of the nature of joy. Here are four suggestions:

Number One: Do something constructive. We have to remember that depression feeds on inertia, and action is the natural enemy of unhappiness. The less we do, the less we want to do. If we want to fight unhappiness, we have to fight inertia. It is important for us to try to make out a plan, a daily series of activities, which takes into account the obvious principle that action always comes before motivation. That is, we must not wait until we feel like doing something to start doing something, because as long as we are unhappy, we will never feel like doing something. The idea is to get moving whether we feel like it or not.

Number Two: Get involved in service. More and more leading members of the psychiatric community understand that altruism is a good way to move towards better health. Volunteer work, community service, but above all, real service in the Church, has a therapeutic effect. Really, we must have compassion and understanding for others before we can get a grip on ourselves, and this is what is meant in the scriptures by finding ourselves by losing ourselves in the service of others. Moreover, because isolation from people is an important cause of depression, and unhappiness and is a result of a kind of backwards arrogance, human contact in and of itself heals us, particularly when we put ourselves in the service of people that we don't think we even like.

Number Three: Schedule joy. Notice that many unhappy people give up the pastimes they enjoy most: this only makes matters worse. We must include in our daily living upbeat activities. Focus on social interactions, especially get-togethers with friends; projects that make us feel competent, such as mastering new skills; service to others, of course; and pleasurable events. We must remember that our behavior shapes our emotions. If we are feeling sad, we actually have to change our behavioral patterns. For example, rather than dragging our feet, walk briskly. Rather than slouching, sit upright. And don't frown: smile, even if we have to look at ourselves in the mirror to see if we look like happy people. If we don't look like a happy people, we must change the way we look, and we will actually begin to become a happy people. The actions that go into being happy, the expressions, the postures, and the movements, help make us feel happy. It is a wonder that people don't grasp this principle taught in the scriptures, which is that our behavior shapes our emotions more than the other way around.

Number Four: Exercise regularly. People who don't exercise regularly will probably never believe this, but it is a fact that aerobic exercise (such as walking, jogging, swimming, bicycling) boosts our self confidence, improves our sense of well-being, and heightens our energy. There are physiological reasons for this and we should remember that any kind of physical exercise, but especially hard physical exercise, followed by a period of rest, can and will reduce the tension and anxiety that contribute to unhappiness and depression.

As a matter of fact, the "mighty change of heart" the scriptures talk about and these practical suggestions for how to help this mighty change by altering behavioral patterns are all part of the emotional growth which is where joy really comes from. Were we more conscious of assessing our emotional growth, we might try more conscientiously to increase our emotional growth into a process of joy on a daily basis. Critical to the development of joy are the management of appetites and passions and the flowering of virtuous emotional qualities. Love, patience, forbearance, and compassion are the essentials of joy. Hatred, envy, lust, and rage must be eradicated from our lives or we will be forever unhappy. Even hatred or envy or lust or rage *to the slightest degree* will give Satan a way to urge us to depression. It has been suggested by the

Brethren since the beginning of this dispensation that there are several kinds of changes we need to make in natural man in order for us to move towards joy and happiness and to get out of unhappiness and depression: these include mutual sacrifice, emotional control, having patience with one another, being a caring and nurturing person, and having a kind of thoughtfulness and consideration for one another. Think of the large number of times that Presidents McKay and Kimball spoke of the kind of emotional control over ourselves that can be gained through three controllable things: namely, courtesy (meaning good manners), even-temperedness, and rejecting self-gratification. All three of these aspects of emotional control have to do with our tendency to gratify our own desires without reference to the desires of others, or to "do our own thing" without reference to enduring social values. Unhappiness is always a matter of self-seeking rather than seeing others served first. There are always those who race to be first, who elbow and push others out of the way (not just physically but emotionally), who serve themselves first at the table, so to speak. These people are not accommodating, caring, nurturing, or thoughtful of others and are, by definition, unhappy.

There is a sure guide to happiness. President McKay said in the general conference of April 1936

> All mankind desires happiness. Many also strive sincerely to make the most and best of themselves. Surprisingly few, however, realize that [the] sure guide to such achievement is found in the following declaration by Jesus of Nazareth: "[Then said Jesus unto his disciples, If any man will come after me, let him deny himself, and take up his cross, and follow me. For] whosoever will save his life shall lose it: and whosoever will lose his life for my sake shall find it. [For what is a man profited, if he shall gain the whole world, and lose his own soul? or what shall a man give in exchange for his soul?" (Matthew 16:24–26)]. This significant passage contains a secret more worthy of possession than fame or dominion, something more valuable than all the wealth of the world.... Why, then, do men and nations ignore a thing so precious? (45)

That is, there is a law which, if lived, inevitably brings joy and happiness to the individual, and if not lived, brings unhappiness and depression. Specifically stated, this is the law: we live our lives most completely and happily when we strive to make the world better and happier for other people. The law of survival of the fittest, of self-preservation at the sacrifice of all else, contrasts to the law of true spirituality and true joy, which is denying self-serving practices in order to serve the good of others. In short, at our most spiritually healthy and emotionally steady, we can only be happy when we serve.

Elder Marion D. Hanks tells the following personal story which illustrates the connection between a mighty change in our hearts, practical service, and happiness.

> I was in the missionary home in Salt Lake City trying to help new missionaries get a sense of their great Christian responsibility when I had a vision of my own. There was a foundation to the vision. The night before in the Salt Lake Tabernacle a man had died of a heart attack while he listened to the choir. He was sitting next to his wife and turned to her as the choir practiced and said "Martha, after all these years, we can be here while the choir practices. You know, I don't have to die to go to heaven to hear the angels. This is enough for me!" He then sat so quietly that she respected his worshipful attention, but, after the rehearsal, when all the others were stirring and moving, and she turned to him, he still didn't move. He had died there on the seat in the tabernacle. Well, I was called, and that night I made a call. I found out that this lady, a crippled person who was quite elderly and walking with a cane, had come with her husband from Los Angeles in fulfillment of a dream. That night, alone and stricken with this tragic thing, she found a place to stay with a considerate choir member, and I tried to do what I could to be helpful. Then I went about my day's activities. The next day I was in the missionary home at four o'clock talking to missionaries as I have said, and as I looked at my watch, I had this little vision, the vision of Mrs. Bernafa, walking by the railing down the ramp of the railroad station while along came a wagon with a box in it I had a picture of her all alone, so I said to the missionaries, "I'm sorry, I must go. I have to go now. God bless you, work hard, and be happy!" I ran out the door, got in my car, raced down to the Union Pacific station, left my car where I should not have left it, jumped over a railing, ran down the ramp, and there saw the picture I had seen before, this elderly woman with a package on one arm and a cane in her hand. Just then the wagon rolled by with the body of her beloved in a box. I took her by the arm and took her to her car, took her to her place in the train, expressed my love and sympathy,

> and went my way. Let me tell you in all sobriety that if you would like to make it a happy day, a good day, get your mind off yourself. Look around you. At moments of depression which is self-centeredness, if you'll follow a simple program you'll get out of it. Get on your knees and get the help of God, then get up and go find somebody who needs something that you can help them find. Then you will be happy. (*Make it a Good Day* 6–7)

Remember the principles of, and suggestions for, true happiness. It will not do to be superficially sentimental, arrogant, indulgent of Satan in his desires. We can *decide* to be happy.

Idea Ten: MARRIAGE

Intimate Custody

The history of the human race can be seen in a most interesting way by reference to marriage and family.

> Scientists today say that civilization is to be measured at different stages largely by the development of the home. Historically they tell us about practices of different forms of marriage among early peoples and races. Such practices as polyandry, polygamy, bigamy, exogamy, monogamy are among them. Most of these investigators are united in the conclusion that the family stands forth as the highest form of associated life. It is the natural unit of all future civic development. (*Secrets of a Happy Life* 13)

Understanding marriage and family life is at the root of our capacity to act in such a way as to assure that we remain a civilized people. Marriage represents custody of the most intimate and important features of human culture. In a work now lost, *On Philosophy*, Aristotle warns against misunderstanding the fact that marriage and family are central to all civilized structure and discourse. Evoking the great cataclysms that cyclically annihilate civilizations, he outlines the process by which survivors must reconstruct human interrelations, turning their attention ultimately to the creation of the *polis* (city), the site of the most extended inter-relational structure. It is in the *polis* that laws and traditions are formed that link complex groups of people together. Such laws and traditions can only originate with *individual* virtues suitable to a citizen, when at crucial points in human history, all aspects of religious, judicial, and social values unite in a common effort. Significantly, Aristotle argues, the *polis* is like an extended family, since it is formed by the merger of villages that themselves are a merger of households. The *oikos* (domestic family unit) is the only natural community, the only one that operates by its very nature not merely from the need to survive biologically, or even economically or socially, but by values that transcend mere biological realities and relationships. The animal world, lower than that of humankind, operates by *biological* imperatives and thus, being without fundamental structures that go beyond, and often cancel out, mere biological kinship, does not exist by *values*. The nuclear human family shares a living communion of values that endows its members with a common identity. For this reason, a violation of communal identity evokes a religious horror, a feeling of defilement. Destruction of the *oikos* by defilement of the values that underlie its reason for being is the ultimate sacrilege. Furthermore, in the nuclear family, any wrong done to a particular individual or to the values that give the unit its meaning, is clearly an attack on all, and is what ultimately requires the *polis* to establish the law and order necessary to the survival of civilization. Marriage and family are the original and final sacrosanct entities that make us human and provide us with a civilization that rises above the level of animal survival.

As many times as Aristotle's argument has been sustained in subsequent centuries by the best thinkers of the human race including recently by family scientists (*Ensign*, August 2001, 29–35), it is vastly more important that God himself has declared the sacred nature of marriage and family. "Marriage between a man and a woman is ordained of God and…the family is central to the Creator's plan for the eternal destiny of His children" (*The Family: A Proclamation to the World*). Of course, human existence being what it is, there "must needs be an opposition in all things" (2 Nephi 2:11), or else the necessary comparison and contrast in human evaluation and decision-making could lead neither to correct understanding of things nor to false judgement. The history of humankind is also, therefore, marked by countless worldly ideas that contradict heavenly declarations, worldly definitions that dilute or even altogether eliminate the God-declared sacredness of marriage and family, notwithstanding the superficial truth of some of them and the sincerity of some of their formulators. God's definitions are absolute: He is not called *Alpha and Omega* in vain. Let us not underestimate how vast is the gap between how the world defines marriage and family on the one hand and what they actually are on the other. To accept either the essence or the implications of worldly notions of marriage and family is to invite disaster of the highest degree, to participate in destroying not only the highest possibilities of human civilization, but also, and more importantly, to participate in the kind of universal fraud that can only lead to eternal destruction. "The disintegration of the family will bring upon individuals, communities, and nations the calamities foretold" by God through His holy prophets since mortality and history began (*The Family: A Proclamation to the World*). The definitions of marriage and family offered by the world and those declared by the Lord are not simply somewhat different—they are absolutely opposed. Significantly, those in the covenant have the absolute obligation to stand in open opposition to the world in these matters. As Moroni says, "Do ye suppose that God will look upon you as guiltless while ye sit still and behold these things? Behold I say unto you, Nay" (Alma 60:23).

I

Marriage is *a man and a woman sealed together for time and for eternity by the power of the Priesthood.* The relationship is *tripartite, egoless, and covenental.* But the world defines marriage as two people consenting to a legal relationship for time. This "marriage" is *bipartite, ego-centered, and contractual.* All three elements of true marriage are subverted or eliminated in the latter view.

A *real* marriage relationship is tripartite: that is, there are three persons involved in three relationships constituting one set of values and agreements, the man with God, the woman with God, and the man with the woman. The relationship is egoless: that is, the man and the woman give up themselves for the sake of the other. And the relationship is covenental: the parties covenant with each other by the power of the Priesthood, not contract with each other by the power of man. The importance of the existence and interpenetration of these elements, and their proper connection with each other for the eternities are often pointed out, for example:

> Whatever honors, privileges, or glory are attained by the man through the Priesthood, are those shared with and enjoyed by the wife...for they are one – inseparably... In other words, the man cannot attain to glory, honor, or exaltation without the woman, nor the woman without the man... While man...is the direct object on whom the power and honor of the Priesthood are bestowed, and he is the active medium of its operations, she partakes of its benefits, its blessings, its powers, its rights and privileges... The power is not given to the woman to act independent of the man, nor is it given to the man to act independent of Christ. (*Truth and Courage* 11–12)

And the Lord has made it perfectly clear why we must make and keep covenants. Covenants show us "the straightness of the path, and the narrowness of the gate, by which (we) should enter" (2 Nephi 31:9), and are the specific means by which we are to keep the commandments and follow the Savior (2 Nephi 31:10). It is through our covenants that we are able to "follow the son, with full purpose of heart, acting no hypocrisy and no deception before God, but with real intent" (2 Nephi 31:13). The covenant-keeping process begins with baptism and the laying on of hands, by those in authority, for the gift of the Holy Ghost, and continues through the remainder of the parts of the New and Everlasting Covenant, including temple sealing, again by those in authority, of man and woman in eternal marriage, all the while giving us the opportunity to see if each of us is a person who "endureth to the end" so that we "shall be saved" (2 Nephi 31:15). We must keep our covenants if we are to find happiness and avoid tragedy. As Heavenly Father has so plainly revealed:

> And as the covenant which they made unto me has been broken, even so it has become void and of none effect. And wo be unto him by whom this offense cometh, for it had been better for him that he had been drowned in the depth of the sea. But blessed are they who have kept the covenant and observed the commandment, for they shall obtain mercy. (*Doctrine and Covenants* 54:4–6)

Remember what the difference between a covenant and a contract is. The first is not negotiable, cannot be terminated at will, is valid for all eternity, and is entered into by Priesthood oath. The second is negotiable, can be terminated under human law, is valid for time only, and is entered into by some recognized legal means, such as a signature or handshake. A true marriage comes by way of covenant: a marriage under the world's laws, no matter how sincerely entered into, will not be a marriage in the hereafter.

Marriage is a laboratory for celestial life. We learn during the mortal segment of our eternal marriages what the purposes are, and how to do the work of, eternal spouses and parents. True marriage provides each partner with the opportunity to become like the Savior; honorable, selfless, intelligent, and giving. Marriage will transform the righteous from creatures of the world, subject to Satan, into children of the Most High, subject to the celestial kingdom's laws of joy. Heavenly Father has standards for marriage, standards often and clearly outlined for the honest seeker and the pure in heart, easily gleaned, for example, from the study guide *Family Relations,* Elder Packer's *Eternal Love,* and Elder Hanks' *Now and Forever.* Close study of the scriptures and these prophetic sources is revealing and thought-provoking.

Parties to the marital covenant are one in the Lord. Such harmony results from Christ-like attitudes and habits on the part of husband and wife. In addition to the central insights offered in sources already mentioned, it may be worth pondering three other factors in marital harmony. First of all, harmony results from a common commitment level and set of behavioral patterns within the Church (not just two people being members of record in the Church). Secondly, harmony is more easily generated when both parties to the marriage come from a common socio-economic background, with common thinking and emotional patterns about work, home life, individual responsibility, and group effort, than is generally the case when such a background is not present. And thirdly, oneness is usually the result when both partners have a relentless, even fierce commitment to open, honest, fearless, and loving communication.

II

The relationship between marriage and family may be stated in this way: *a family is the unit created by marriage*. When a man and a woman are sealed together for time and eternity in a temple, a marriage is performed and *a new family is created*. It is crucial to recognize that the family is created by the power of the Priesthood; thus, a family, in the eternal sense, is a *covenental* relationship, not a *biological* one. It is common in the world to think of a family as a biological unit resulting from sexual relations, but this definition is at best problematic and at worst an egregious falsehood, because it may lead us to valorize biological relationships over covenental ones, thus subverting the Lord's purposes. In this light we may wish to be careful about phrases such as "families are forever." Such statements may not reflect the implications of Priesthood covenants. Consider this way of stating the facts: biological families *can become* covenant families *if* their members *make* covenants, and covenant families *can be* together forever *if* their members *keep* their covenants.

Achieving a high degree of celestiality in our families is possible, and has been spoken of by Heavenly Father through the scriptures and the mouths of his prophets since the beginning. "If we really try, our home can be a bit of heaven here on earth. The thoughts we think, the deeds we do, the lives we live, influence not only the success of our earthly journey; they mark the way to our eternal goals" (President Thomas S. Monson, *Ensign*, November 1988, 69). The process begins in this way: "If you build your homes on the foundation rock of our Redeemer and the gospel, they can be sanctuaries where your families can be sheltered from the raging storms of life" (Elder Joseph B. Wirthlin, *Ensign*, May 1993, 71). Celestial families begin with husbands and wives sharing responsibility for ensuring that daily family prayer, scripture study, and group work effort are cheerfully done, and that regular attendance at Church meetings is an integral part of the family fabric. Husbands and wives work together in teaching children and, when necessary, disciplining them. Wise marriage partners will allow their individual characteristics and abilities to complement each other. And one of the greatest foundation blocks for a powerful family life is loyalty: as President Gordon B. Hinckley has said, "Determine that there will never be anything that will come between you that will disrupt your marriage. Make it work. Resolve to make it work. There is far too much of divorce, wherein hearts are broken and sometimes lives are destroyed. Be fiercely loyal one to another" (*Ensign*, February 1999, 2–4).

Rearing children is the chief work of a family created by the Lord in the temple. Children are part of an earthly family on a custodial basis only: God was their parent before we were and He has given up neither His rights nor His interest (see President Gordon B. Hinckley, *Ensign*, July 1997, 73). "In many ways earthly parents represent their Heavenly Father in the process of nurturing, loving, caring, and teaching children. Children naturally look to their (earthly) parents to learn of the characteristics of their Heavenly Father" (Bishop Robert D. Hales, *Ensign*, November 1993, 9). Children are *entitled* to a loving and learning relationship with their parents, one that is based upon President Brigham Young's counsel: "Bring up your children in the love and fear of the Lord; study their dispositions and their temperaments, and deal with them accordingly..." (*Discourses of Brigham Young*, 207). A number of resources are available for families in their quest for greater happiness, for truer fidelity as parents and children, including the *Family Guidebook*, the *Family Home Evening Resource Book*, and *A Parent's Guide*. Their proper use is highly recommended and will change all concerned for the better.

Idea Eleven: DIVORCE

Infinite Perfidy

Sadly, not all families survive the onslaughts of the world's ways and may limp along in disarray or even end in divorce. Divorce is *always* the result of transgression: it is not part of the Gospel plan. And a divorce does not just "happen:" it is *the personal choice by one of the marriage partners to leave the family.* Recall what a family is: by definition, one cannot leave just the marriage and somehow stay in the family. The world would have us believe that divorce is simply the dissolution of the "marriage" contract by process of the world's law, where in the aftermath everybody involved can learn to "get along with each other," behave as though nothing at the root of eternal life has happened and, above all, not treat it as evil but in a "non-judgmentally" shoulder-shrugging way. This is a horribly disturbed attitude that does not take into consideration the *point* of marriage in the first place, which is: unless we secure our covenants by the sealing power of the Priesthood, *and stay in those covenants,* then "in the life to come we shall have neither father, mother, brother, sister, wife, children, not friends... [and all our] contracts, covenants, bonds, obligations, oaths, vows, connections, and associations are dissolved in the grave..." (President Joseph F. Smith, *The Deseret News*, 11 November 1873, 1). And a great Old Testament story illustrates just what this means (I Chronicles 5:1). Reuben had the birthright in his family but, by the act of committing sexual sin, *by definition* he gave it up. God therefore gave the birthright to Joseph. But most significantly, Reuben could never get the birthright back again and, in addition, *he was never called "father" in Israel again*." When one gives up his/her place, he/she *cannot* get it back. It has been given to another. That is, every covenant we betray or leave, by transgression or abandonment, results in dissolution forever of all personal associations connected to that covenant. This is what covenant abandonment does. This is what divorce *is*.

And in any case, abandonment of the covenant is the counterforce to marriage, is never a cure for anything, and is only a temporary escape (*Marriage and Divorce* 14). So why, we may ask, is divorce so rampant? Satan knows that marriage and family are absolutely central to the very reason for mortal existence, so his need to be influential in betrayal and divorce is clear. From the eternal point of view, divorce is the ultimate familial crisis because it is nothing less than the willful destruction of a family. Covenant-betrayers and divorce-filers involve themselves in numerous fallacies in order to try to justify their destructive decisions and behaviors through a process of redefinition or tempering of God's pronouncements. And every divorce-filer is certain that his/her reasons for violating the covenant are valid—he/she is the "exception" to God's rules. It is alarming that we sometimes go along with these misconceptions: when we do, we muddy the clarity of Gospel principles and slip away into the malicious mire of the Adversary's definitional traps. Here are eight of the most destructive fallacies:

Fallacy One. The "It Takes Two To Tango" fallacy asserts that in any divorce, by definition *both* spouses are in some way at fault. This is nonsensical on the face of it. There is no such thing as "group" will: in a marriage one person is always the first to begin considering covenant violation, whether it is committing adultery, filing for divorce from an innocent person, or something like unto these things. And, in any case, marriage partners cannot break their covenants at exactly the same instant, at exactly the same moment of decision, given the complexity of individuality. Furthermore, at any given moment along the way to divorce, *one* of the partners inevitably is more willing to keep the marriage going than the other. It is relatively easy to tell who is responsible for the evil of divorce:

> For I say unto you that whatsoever is good cometh from God, and whatsoever is evil cometh from the devil. Therefore, if a man bringeth forth good works he hearkeneth unto the voice of the good shepherd, and he doth follow him: but whosoever bringeth forth evil works, the same becometh a child of the devil, for he hearkeneth unto his voice, and doth follow him. (Alma 5:40–1)

Of course, in its typical drive to make everyone party to group guilt, the world calls this point of view "simple-minded."

Fallacy Two. The "Irreconcilable Differences" fallacy asserts that in any divorce, by definition *nobody* is at fault. This fallacy is so obviously false that it would be comical if it did not find such a prominent place in divorce-excuses today. According to this fallacy, both spouses are just fine, but they "just cannot seem to get along together" or "since people are all different, we can expect that some relationships just will not last." The fact is that there is no such thing as an "irreconcilable difference," only a difference for which one of the spouses *refuses* to make a change. Under the covenant, anything a spouse has to do in order to come into conformity with God's marriage pattern *can* be done, including major attitude and behavioral changes, *if* humility and contrition are present to replace the pride at the root of adultery, divorce-filing, and other covenant-breaking actions. Only the proud find differences "irreconcilable."

Fallacy Three. The "It Must Have Been Wrong From The Beginning" error would have us accept the idea that a divorce can come about because there is something so determinate about a spouse's human weaknesses that nothing can ever change them into marriage-compatible strengths. Any man and any woman can have a good marriage if they both decide to live the Gospel and stick to it no matter what happens. To redefine the beginnings of a marriage in such a way as to justify later divorce is the kind of *post hoc* thinking that is the mark of the weak-minded.

Fallacy Four. The "Men Are Usually The Cause" deception seems to be the legacy of pent-up frustration over the tragic masculism marking so much of the history of various world cultures. The fact is, there is no hard evidence that in our society divorce is caused by the male more than by the female partner. The problem is that cross-gender blaming is rampant in Satan's world, and is part of his method of destroying charity and understanding. Unfortunately, we often participate in this fraud by using as general causal examples in divorce a male figure, by which process we demonize men and continue to treat women as though they were preternally innocent, passive, without volition, and incapable of choice.

Fallacy Five. The "It Is Just Between The Spouses" illusion has extremely tragic consequences. Divorce does not simply end a relationship between spouses: it destroys the eternal unit God ordained never to be destroyed. Thus, divorce destroys the bond of identity and nurture ordained to reside in the husband and wife as one unit, the bond that children, extended family, and the whole *polis* relies upon for its order and health. The devilish sinfulness that leads a spouse to forget that he/she has promised to stay in the covenant, has devastatingly negative consequences in the lives *of all others* concerned. "Thus we see how quick the children of men do forget the Lord their God, yea, how quick to do iniquity, and to be led away by the evil one. Yea, and we also see the great wickedness one very wicked man can cause to take place among the children of men" (Alma 46:8–9). Such wickedness on the part of the covenant-breaking spouse works a powerful negative effect on children, not only by setting up an evil example, but also by tending to cancel out what the righteous parent is teaching and exemplifying, a consequence for the covenant-breaker that will bring about inevitable eternal torment (Alma 39:11). Divorce does not destroy a marriage only: it destroys an entire family.

Fallacy Six. The "It Is The Result Of Conflict Between People" fallacy would have us believe that conflict *in and of itself* is determinate in interpersonal relationships. Of course, it is nothing of the sort. The fact that people do not always harmonize on things is the result of the fact that people are individuals, not group clones. That there is potential or actual conflict between people has nothing to do with whether those people get along and even thrive: the only relevant factor is what people decide to do about the conflict. The point is that conflict does not cause divorce: a spouse's refusal to deal with the conflict in a Christ-like manner and according to the counsel of Priesthood leaders is the problem. Studies have shown that there is equal conflict between people who divorce and those who stay married. Divorce is caused by a spouse who wants to get out of the marriage for whatever reason, using "conflict" as an excuse.

Fallacy Seven. The "Devil Made Me Do It" sophistry is the contradiction in a spouse's claim that in some way God has authorized him/her to seek a divorce or to break the covenant in some other way. God cannot authorize the destruction of something He has already set up as permanent. Someone who says that she/he "prayed about it" and got an answer that he/she should file for divorce from a non-excommunicatable person may well have received revelation on the matter, but it is all too obvious where such a revelation came from. A person can destroy a marriage that God, for His own reasons, at some later time may cancel the sealing of, but it is profane and emotionally-disturbed to claim that God authorized the divorce or other covenant-breaking act, especially "before the fact."

Fallacy Eight. The "It Did Not Work Out Because Of A Partner's Weakness" excuse is another one of those silly nonsensicalities that are false *prima facia.* Everybody has weaknesses: therefore, if weaknesses were a reason for divorce, all marriages would be doomed from the beginning. This fallacy seems to be the result of a misunderstanding of perfectibility, patience, forbearance, and God's plan for our eternal joy. And it may be worth noting that many people who indulge in this fallacy are those who are quicker to find the mote in others than the beam in themselves. And in any case, no person *causes* another to break the covenant, for example by committing adultery or by filing for divorce. God is very clear on this matter:

> ... if they are condemned they bring upon themselves their own condemnation. And now remember, remember... that whosoever perisheth, perisheth unto himself; and whosoever doeth iniquity, doeth it unto himself; for behold, ye are free; ye are permitted to act for yourselves; for behold, God hath given unto you a knowledge and he hath made you free. He hath given unto you that ye might know good from evil, and he hath given unto you that ye might choose life or death; and ye can do good and be restored unto that which is good, or have that which is good restored unto you; or ye can do evil, and have that which is evil restored unto you. (Helaman 14: 29–31)

When a person commits adultery or abandons a marriage by divorcing a person innocent of such a crime, that person has violated the covenant by her/his own unrighteousness, and not because somehow he/she was "forced" into it. When a person finds herself/himself unhappy and seeking a "way out" of the covenant, we can be sure that "they brought upon themselves the curse...and even so doth every man that is cursed bring upon himself his own condemnation" (Alma 3:19).

IV

It is difficult to imagine anything as profound and joyous as real marriage. It is likewise difficult to imagine any series of events caused by human choice that is so relentlessly devastating as divorce. In this regard, it is important to note that the act of filing for divorce is in and of itself and by definition the violation of the covenant, the breaking of the promise made to never break the promise. But Heavenly Father has revealed that, *under very exceptional circumstances*, there are grounds for the cancellation of a sealing (*Secrets of a Happy Life* 35). Such extreme circumstances do not include hurt feelings, depression, exaggerated difficulties with a spouse, self-justification or scapegoating for one's transgressions, going away to "find oneself," and so on. And notice that it is not the divorce-filer's right to decide if legitimate circumstances for a cancellation obtain, since she/he has a personal stake in assessing blame. That is, a spouse who judges his/her partner to be "divorceable" is making only an interior judgment, and also is not called by the Lord to an ecclesiastical position to make such a judgment: the arrogance of making judgments about the covenant without Priesthood authority severely compounds the already Satanic effects of the divorce decision itself. Only the Eternal Being has the power and authority to dissolve a covenant (since the covenant itself transcends this life and is entered into by His rules), so only His grounds for requesting dissolution have any validity. And even when it has been judged that any of these grounds are present, there is no *automatic* presumption of ecclesiastical dissolution.

The first of these grounds is sexual misconduct, often defined as the only ground, and involves violating any aspect of the law of chastity, such as adultery (sexual relations with someone to whom one is not married), "reverse" adultery (refusal to have sexual relations with the person to whom one is married), homosexuality, and the like. A second possible ground is murder. A third is abandonment which includes such actions as dereliction of spousal or parental duty, (refusal to provide and share physical, emotional, and communicative intimacy, resources, and tasks), providing and sharing intimacy to others secretively outside the marriage, and leaving the marriage by filing for divorce. A fourth is sin against the Holy Ghost (open rebellion against the Church, its authorities, and Gospel doctrines, as well as actively or passively subverting righteousness in others). In fact, it seems clear that all these grounds are types of *infidelity* and, further, that any kind of abuse, active or passive, falls into this category.

Sexual sin seems to be the chief cause of family disaster, and it cannot be condemned in too strong terms. God has commanded us (*Doctrine and Covenants* 42:22–4) to love our spouses with all our hearts, cleaving unto him/her and none else. Even to "look upon" another of the opposite sex is to "deny the faith" and to "lose the Spirit." To refuse to repent of adultery or "lusting after" another means to be cast out of the covenant. And it is crucial to note how sexual sin and abandonment often go hand-in-hand. The Lord puts it this way:

> Behold, verily I say unto you, that whatever persons among you, having put away their companions for the cause of fornication, or in other words, if they shall testify before you in all lowliness of heart that this is the case, ye shall not cast them out from among you; but if ye shall find that any persons have left their companions for the sake of adultery, and they themselves are the offenders, and their companions are living, they shall be cast out from among you." (*Doctrine and Covenants* 42:74–5)

A person may rightly ask for an adulterous spouse to be "put away," but a person who is herself/himself the offender, in sexual or other matters, is under the most severe condemnation for trying to scapegoat the innocent spouse. Abandonment by filing for divorce from a spouse who has not committed adultery is the most common tactic of the covenant-breaker.

IV

When a new sealing is set to take place, and an ecclesiastical cancellation is given, one family unit is at an end, a new family unit is to be created, and a change has taken place in the celestial *polis*. Family members have special responsibilities as regards this change. Remember that a family is a covenant relationship under God's rules, not a contract relationship under the world's direction. Its standards are not determined by the way the world and its institutions think and feel about things, or how they define things, but by the way in which the Gospel directs thinking and feeling about things. For this reason, the fundamental responsibility of every member of a family is the same as it is for every person in any other part of the New and Everlasting Covenant, whether it be baptism, receipt of Priesthood authority, or whatever. That responsibility is to *become converted.* That is, every person within a Priesthood covenant has as his or her most fundamental responsibility to become converted to the requirements of the relationships in *that covenant.* This is a choice to be made by husband and wife, the children of the covenant, extended family members, and all others. When a sealing is cancelled, that is, when an original covenant no longer exists, the dissolution of the covenant by definition ends one family, and the new covenant into which the innocent party enters begins another. This new family requires all involved to *become converted* just as any covenant does.

It is important to remember what *conversion* is, to put into practice the characteristics and behaviors that distinguish people who are truly converted. Think of a person who has spent many years working for, say, the Ajax Food Company. His entire attitude, his feelings, his conceptions about work and work relationships are fixed upon that company. Then he finds another job at the Acme Office Products Company. If he is going to be an employee of the Acme Company, he is not going to get up every morning, load his briefcase with Ajax materials, and go to the Ajax building to work! He is going to have to leave that all behind, and fix his attention on the Acme Company. He is now under contract to the Acme company, and the Ajax Company *no longer has any call on his loyalty*. He may remember his days with his first company, he may maintain a friendly attitude towards the first company, and he may keep in mind that he has learned much there: but his loyalty and effort are now to be given in their entirety to his new company. In short, he must *become converted* to the new company which means, by definition, that he must *leave behind* the old company. If he does not, his is a weak and untrustworthy character. Conversion in covenant matters is the same, except far more important and far more revelatory of a person's true character. When a person, for example, joins the Church, his is the responsibility to become *converted to* the Gospel, to the principles and procedures of the Church of Jesus Christ of Latter-day Saints. He may maintain friendly relations with people in his previous congregation, and he may remember his many years there and what he has learned, but his entire loyalty, his entire effort, his feelings and his patterns of thinking are now to be given to the Church. He must *leave behind* the entire complex of attitudes, feelings, and assumptions of the past, and be a Latter-day Saint. Until he becomes a Latter-day Saint *all the way*, he is not converted and cannot be entrusted with the higher things of the Spirit. It is interesting in this regard to review the way the Anti-Nephi-Lehis showed that they were truly converted (Alma 23-29), and to ask ourselves what they teach us about being so converted that they left *everything* behind and "never did fall away" from their new covenant family.

There seems to be little understanding in the world that *conversion* is exactly what is at stake in family relationships. When the Lord creates a family by sealing two faithful covenant-keepers in the remainder of the New and Everlasting Covenant (temple sealing) all members of that family are under the strictest and most sacred obligation to *become converted to* that family, that covenant. That is why both man and woman must *leave behind* their biological father and mother's family and *become converted* to their new family. Remember that ultimately we are children in our mother and father's family, not because we were biological offspring (that is the world's way of defining it), but because we were born within the sealing of two people who happen to be our biological forebears. We are not children of parents because we are biologically related, and we are not husband and wife because we are biologically related: we are children of parents because we are sealed into a patriarchal covenant line, and we are husband and wife because we are sealed into a patriarchal covenant line. Biological relationships are earthly; covenant relationships are eternal. We must *become converted* to our covenant relationships, *leaving behind*, if necessary, those that are biological only.

As raw as it seems, and as terrible as divorce is, especially on children, all involved must stop acting as though life is over. It is important to face the reality that previous covenant relationships are at an end, and this is so because of the actions of the covenant-breaker, for whom the original covenant and its dominion can never be retrieved. As God puts it: "behold his mission is given unto him, and it shall not be given again" (D&C 58:16). Our covenant responsibilities are given and they must be met: if they are not met and the covenant is cancelled, the relationships set in place by that covenant are gone and will not be given again. Other covenants can be entered into, but the particular blessings and relationships of former covenants cannot be received.

Now it would be wonderful if it happens that our biological relationships parallel our covenant relationships through a process of everyone from Adam and Eve down through all human history making and keeping the New and Everlasting Covenant. But it seems obviously not the case; not everyone will accept and make these covenants, and of those who do, not everyone will keep them. This is sad, even tragic. Nevertheless, the test of our character is whether or not we put our energy, our feelings, our devotions, and our loyalty into our covenant relationships, instead of valorizing biological relationships and neglecting or even stubbornly refusing the blessings the covenant and its valiant members have to offer. The covenant we are in, held inviolate by righteous covenant-keepers, is the issue: the covenant that once was, but has been, for reasons of spousal wickedness, cancelled, is past and will never be put into place again. Dealing with this is a matter of maturity, of being emotionally grown up enough to cease living in the dream-world of the past.

Dealing with the perfidy of divorce is also a matter of responsibility. The wronged parent has a special responsibility to avoid acting as though "everything is okay," that the past has an absolute present validity, or that the covenant-breaking spouse is guiltless. The children have the responsibility to stop living in that dream-world of the past, pretending that biological relationships are as important (or even supercede!) covenant ones, to live in the covenant relationships of the present, to support righteousness and those who try to do what is right, and to take an open and public stance against evil and evil-doers. Children must remember that just because someone had sexual intercourse with his/her father/mother it does not make him/her the parent. Extended family members have the special responsibility to support those in the newly-constituted family.

In other words, if, through the sins of sexual deviation, abandonment, or felony, a previously sealed covenant relationship is cancelled by

Priesthood authorities, all parties touched by the cancellation must *leave behind* the old and *become converted* to any newly created sealing. Husbands and wives in the newly sealed relationship are a family, just as if they had been together from the first. The old is wiped away, the new is forever. Children will be placed in a patriarchal line of those who have kept the covenant and no longer are under any *family* obligation to those who did not keep the covenant. Like the person who was reared in a different church, children may remember the past, maintain charity and hope for those left behind, and respect good things learned, but their entire loyalty, their whole complex of feelings and thinking patterns are now to be given to the new family. To try to somehow straddle a fence between two groups of people, one of which is now the family and the other which is not (even though there are biological connections) is the same thing as to be baptized into the Church of Jesus Christ of Latter-day Saints but still try to maintain membership in a counter organization. It is loyalty to the world rather than to the Gospel that invites such straddling, and calls into question the level of commitment a person has to the gospel imperative to leave the world and take upon oneself the whole plan of steadfastness and consecration.

Consecration works. Marriage is an oath and a promise, and keeping that promise brings a miracle of joy and growth. But breaking that promise brings a disaster of destruction that only repentance and conversion can heal.

Idea Twelve: CONSEQUENCES

The Law of the Harvest

One of Satan's greatest deceptions is a point-of-view that has the following four constituent parts: 1. I am just the way I am and I cannot help it; 2. I cannot change the way I am; 3. therefore, others are obligated to accept me as I am; 4. and I am obligated to accept all others for who they are. As has been pointed out in earlier chapters, all four of these premises are false. This kind of thinking leads to spiritual, emotional, and intellectual helplessness. It ignores the two most fundamental issues of humanness revealed in the Gospel: the purpose of life is to *change* for the better, and it is not acceptable to tolerate evil doing.

The Gospel has the antidote to this deception, perhaps seen clearly in this way. It would be shocking folly for a farmer to believe that he could wish a crop into existence, or that he could harvest where nothing has been worked. The spiritual truth of this matter is stated with great power in the New Testament:

> Be not deceived; God is not mocked: for whatsoever a man soweth, that shall he also reap. For he that soweth to his flesh shall of the flesh reap corruption; but he that soweth to the spirit shall of the Spirit reap life everlasting. (Galatians 6:7–8)

All principles of truth, goodness, and beauty are governed by this law of the harvest. Indeed, our involvement in the great conflict of the premortal world, in which our eternal happiness was at stake, turned at its very center on the basic issue of this law, of choice and consequence (Moses 4:3). Heavenly Father taught us that agency or, in other words, choice and consequence, was the key to our eternal growth.

> Next to the bestowal of life itself, the right to direct that life is God's greatest gift to man. Among the immediate obligations and duties resting upon members of the Church today, and one of the most urgent and pressing for attention and action of all liberty-loving people, is the preservation of individual liberty. Freedom of choice is more to be treasured than any possession earth can give… (David O. McKay, *Conference Report*, April 1950, 32)

We are here in mortality *specifically* to make choices.

Now, when we make a choice we also choose its consequences. When we choose poorly, we reap bad consequences and limit our freedom, just as when we choose wisely we reap good consequences and increase our freedom. Think of how sins such as selfishness, sexual immorality, the use of drugs, idleness, avarice, and so on, affect people. Consider how virtues such as integrity, covenant-keeping, and other matters discussed in the preceding essays free us from eternal limitations. It should be obvious that each choice we make gives us freedom to choose additional freedom in the eternities or else the slavery of spiritual captivity. President Gordon B. Hinckley notes that the law of the harvest governs personal success and happiness in this life as well as in the next:

> I remember one weekend when my wife and I visited good friends who live in a rural community in the West. We spent one afternoon driving around the small but attractive farming town, enjoying the tidy homes and cultivated fields nearby. As we mingled with the people, it was obvious that they were unpretentious and principled. They

> had learned from experience that we do not reap wheat after sowing oats, that we cannot get a racehorse from a scrub mare. (*Standing For Something,* 81)

I

The law of the harvest, then, is simply this: you reap what you sow. This law is inviolate in the eternities. It is possible that the reaping will come a long time after the sowing, but it *shall come.* And the harvest often comes relatively soon after the planting. Given the inevitability of this law, it is well to understand six principles embedded in its core.

Principle One. We must plant something in order to reap something. "...whatsoever ye sow, that shall ye also reap... (*Doctrine and Covenants* 6:33). We may fast and pray for sun and rain, we may cultivate and fertilize, and we may work as hard as anyone has ever worked in a field: but if we have not planted seed, nothing will grow.

Principle Two. We cannot reap something different than what we sow. If we want to harvest wheat, we cannot begin by planting oats. We may end up with a wonderful crop of oats, but oats are not wheat. *No matter how good the oat crop is, if we need wheat we are essentially without anything, just as if no crop at all had been planted.* And if the wrong crop has been planted, eventually we will not be able to cover up our mistake. This is true in the spiritual realm as well:

> For a good tree bringeth not forth corrupt fruit; neither doth a corrupt tree bring forth good fruit. For every tree is known by his own fruit. For of thorns men do not gather figs, nor of a bramble bush gather they grapes. (Luke 6:43–44)

Principle Three. We must take care of what we sow. Think of the connection between this principle and the first two in this way:

> Now therefore thus saith the Lord of hosts; consider your ways. Ye have sown much, and bring in little; ye eat, but ye have not enough; ye drink, but ye are not filled with drink; ye clothe you, but there is none warm; and he that earneth wages earneth wages to put it into a bag with holes. (Haggai 1:5–6)

We may very carefully study what kind of seed would best suit our needs and the ground into which it will be planted, and we may fast and pray for its good growth and bountiful harvest, but if we do not do everything we can in order to insure that it will develop into a bounty, then we will end up with very little or nothing at all.

Principle Four. If we work as hard as we can, we shall reap more than we have sown. This is a miracle, but it is true. "But this I say, He which soweth sparingly shall reap also sparingly; and he which soweth bountifully shall reap also bountifully...(and) multiply your seed sown, and increase the fruits of your righteousness" (II Corinthians 9:6–10). If we do the best we can, our efforts will be magnified as much as a hundredfold; if we do not, and "sow the wind," we shall reap not only more wind but a terrible whirlwind (Hosea 8:7).

Principle Five. We cannot reap until the season is come. Patience is required, endurance is required, and a clear understanding of a crop's readiness to be harvested is necessary. "And let us not be weary in well doing; for in due season we shall reap, if we faint not" (Galatians 6:9). If we pick a field of corn before it is ripe, most of our hard work is subverted.

Principle Six. We always get what we want. If we *really* want something, nothing will deter us from doing all it takes to get it. Ponder the words of Alma to his son:

> And it is requisite with the justice of God that men should be judged according to their works; and if their works were good in this life, and the desires of their hearts were good, that they should also, at the last day, be restored unto that which is good. And if their works are evil they shall be restored unto them for evil. Therefore, all things shall be restored to their proper order, every thing to its natural frame—mortality raised to immortality, corruption to incorruption—raised to endless happiness to inherit the kingdom of God, or to endless misery to inherit the kingdom of the devil, the one on the one hand, the other on the other—the one raised to happiness according to his desires of happiness, or good according to his desires of good; and the other to evil according to his desires of evil; for as he has desired to do evil all the day long even so shall he have his reward of evil when the night cometh. (Alma 41:3–5)

If we want happiness, we shall do those things whose ultimate consequence is eternal happiness. If we have not done those things, and we really want eternal joy, we will repent, and no pains of repentance will be too much for us to bear: indeed, we will welcome them. The point is, *a person who does not repent simply does not want happiness.*

II

The law of the harvest is an absolute law that can be neither contravened nor ignored. Planting, working, and harvesting will go on forever, and may involve a certain amount of pain (as hard work usually does), so it is crucial to think about the relationship between *work* and *pain*, between the effort it takes to harvest a worthwhile crop and the sweat, pain, and even agony that can be associated with that effort. And spiritual farming is no easier than cultivating any crop. That is, in order to harvest we must put in the full sweat and effort required by the crop and its circumstances, and this is normally accompanied by varying degrees of pain. We might remember that pain and discomfort are an inevitable part of this life and, like the law of the harvest, of which they are a part, cannot be contravened or ignored. There is no escaping pain, since mortality involves pain at every level.

The point is that ultimately there are only two kinds of pain, the *pain of discipline* and the *pain of regret.* We can choose which one we want. This means, for example, that if we have something important to do as regards cultivating our spiritual crop and we do not do it, we usually experience no pain at that moment (except, perhaps, for a little guilt), because the consequences of our sloth or rebellion quite possibly will come not now, but later. This is why it seems easier to neglect our home teaching, our well-prepared family home evenings, our kind word to a neighbor, and so on, because so doing may not hurt immediately. But if we have something important to do as regards our spiritual harvest and we actually do it, then we experience the pain at that moment associated with the hard work and self-discipline that is always part of the law of the harvest. This decision seems more difficult than the first, because the effects are felt immediately, and it is a condition of the "natural man" that we tend to try to escape from immediate painful consequences if we can.

The first choice relieves us of immediate pain, but the pain that comes later is the inevitable and irreversible consequence of our choice to avoid the work and self-discipline demanded by the purposes of mortality. The absolute result is *regret*, a looking back at the unfortunate past and not being able to change it, an indulgence in sentiments such as "had I only," or "I wish I would have." These feelings will stay with us throughout the eternities.

The second choice allows us to feel the immediate consequences of self-discipline, even though we often do not see the future benefits of our choice right away. But when we cultivate our fields, in the Lord's way and right away, this sort of pain is soon replaced by long-term joy. Those who do not discipline themselves to do what they are expected by the Lord to do, and when He expects them to do it, will, for a short time, have the passing pleasures of life, and then face the eternal consequences of their neglect and rebellion, the everlasting pains of regret.

We cannot postpone the work and self-discipline it takes, at the time it is required, if we are going to have a full harvest. And think of this: *even the pain of discipline gives us the immediate soothing feeling of joy that comes from knowing we are doing the right thing.* Only in this way can we harvest in full the good things we actually planted and cultivated.

III

The immutability of the law of the harvest is one of the most neglected truths of our time. It is astonishing how many of us believe that we are going to "get away with" that which is not authorized by God. In the sermon on the mount, the Savior taught that a city on a hill cannot be hid: that is, what a city ultimately is cannot be disguised. The same is true of every mortal individual (Matthew 5:14–16). When it comes time for us to walk among the rows of spiritual plantings in the fields of our mortal probation, our crop will be bountiful, or it will not. And at the moment of harvest, all the wishing, excuse-making, scapegoating, and protesting will make not the least bit of difference in our fields if we have not observed the principles of the law of the harvest: we shall have very little or nothing for all eternity.

Works Cited

Conference Reports. Salt Lake City: The Church of Jesus Christ of Latter-day Saints, 1899 ff.

The Deseret News. Salt Lake City: Deseret News Publishing Company, 1964 ff.

Dew, Sheri L. *Gordon B. Hinckley: Go Forward With Faith.* Salt Lake City: Deseret Book, 1996.

The Ensign. Salt Lake City: The Church of Jesus Christ of Latter-day Saints, 1971 ff.

The Family: A Proclamation to the World. Salt Lake City: The Church of Jesus Christ of Latter-day Saints, 1995.

Family Guidebook. Salt Lake City: The Church of Jesus Christ of Latter-day Saints, n.d.

Family Home Evening Resource Book. Salt Lake City: The Church of Jesus Christ of Latter-day Saints, n.d.

Family Relations. Salt Lake City: The Church of Jesus Christ of Latter-day Saints, 1975.

Gospel Principles. Salt Lake City: The Church of Jesus Christ of Latter-day Saints, 1995.

Hanks, Marion D. *Now and Forever.* Salt Lake City: Bookcraft, 1974.

Hinckley, Gordon B. *Standing for Something.* New York: Random House, 2000.

Hunter, Howard W. *That We Might Have Joy.* Salt Lake City: Deseret Book, 1994.

The Improvement Era. Salt Lake City: The Church of Jesus Christ of Latter-day Saints, 1897–1971.

Kimball, Spencer W. *Faith Precedes the Miracle.* Salt Lake City: Deseret Book, 1972.

——. *Marriage and Divorce.* Salt Lake City: Deseret Book, 1976.

Lundwall, N. B. *Masterful Discourses and Writings of Orson Pratt.* Salt Lake City: Bookcraft, 1962.

McConkie, Bruce R. *Doctrines of Salvation: Sermons and Writings of Joseph Fielding Smith.* Salt Lake City: Bookcraft, 1998.

McConkie, Joseph Fielding. *Truth and Courage: The Joseph F. Smith Letters.* Cited in *Teachings of Presidents of the Church: Joseph F. Smith.* Salt Lake City: The Church of Jesus Christ of Latter-day Saints, 1998.

McKay, David O. *Secrets of a Happy Life*. Salt Lake City: Bookcraft, 1967.

McKay, Llewelyn R. *True to the Faith: Sermons and Writings of David O. McKay*. Salt Lake City: Bookcraft, 1966.

Melchizedek Priesthood Personal Study Guides. Salt Lake City: The Church of Jesus Christ of Latter-day Saints, 1988–91.

Middlemiss, Claire. *Teachings of President David O. McKay*. Salt Lake City: Deseret Book, 1967.

Packer, Boyd K. *Eternal Love*. Salt Lake City: Deseret Book, 1973.

——. *The Holy Temple*. Salt Lake City: Bookcraft, 1982.

A Parent's Guide. Salt Lake City: The Church of Jesus Christ of Latter-day Saints, 1985.

Peer, Larry H. *Readings on the Rim*. Ann Arbor: Erudition, 2003.

Richards, LeGrand. *A Marvelous Work and a Wonder.* Salt Lake City: Deseret Book, 1976.

Roberts, B. H. *A Comprehensive History of the Church of Jesus Christ of Latter-day Saints.* Provo: Brigham Young University Press, 1965.

Sayers, Dorothy L. *Introductory Papers.* London: Methuen, 1954.

Smith, Joseph Fielding. *Teachings of the Prophet Joseph Smith.* Salt Lake City: Deseret News Press, 1942.

Speeches of the Year. Provo: Brigham Young University, 1966 ff.

The Standard Works: The Holy Bible, The Book of Mormon, The Doctrine and Covenants, The Pearl of Great Price. Salt Lake City: The Church of Jesus Christ of Latter-day Saints, 1988.

Talmage, James E. *The Articles of Faith*. Salt Lake City: The Church of Jesus Christ of Latter-day Saints, 1968.

Teachings of the Presidents of the Church: Harold B. Lee. Salt Lake City: The Church of Jesus Christ of Latter-day Saints, 2000.

Walcott, Derek. *Collected Poems 1948–1984*. New York: Farrar, Straus & Giroux, 1986.

Widtsoe, John A. *Discourses of Brigham Young.* Salt Lake City: Deseret News Press, 1925.

Young Woman's Journal. Salt Lake City: The Church of Jesus Christ of Latter-day Saints, 1889–1929.